Primary Design and Technology for the Future

Creativity, Culture and Citizenship

'023

WN

Alan Howe, Dan Davies and Ron Ritchie

YORK ST. JOHN
COLLEGE LIBRARY

David Fulton Publishers
London

York St. John College

3 8025 00493183 1

David Fulton Publishers Ltd
The Chiswick Centre, 414 Chiswick High Road, London W4 5TF
www.fultonpublishers.co.uk

First published in Great Britain in 2001 by David Fulton Publishers

Note: The rights of Alan Howe, Dan Davies and Ron Ritchie to be
identified as the authors of this work have been asserted by them in accordance
with the Copyright, Designs and Patents Act 1988.

David Fulton Publishers is a division of Granada Learning Limited, part of
Granada plc.

Copyright © Alan Howe, Dan Davies and Ron Ritchie 2001

British Library Cataloguing in Publication Data
A catalogue record for this book is available from the British Library.

ISBN 1-85346-738-3

Pages from this book may be photocopied for use only in purchasing
institution. Otherwise, all rights reserved. No part of this publication may be
reproduced, stored in a retieval system or transmitted, in any form or by any
means, electronic, mechanical, photocopying, or otherwise, without the prior
permission of the publishers.

Typeset by Elite Typesetting Techniques, Eastleigh, Hampshire
Printed and bound in Great Britain

Contents

Notes on contributors   v

Acknowledgements   vi

Introduction   1

Section One: Creativity through design and technology for pupils and teachers

Chapter 1.1: What is creativity?   11
Chapter 1.2: Teaching for creativity and teaching creatively   18
Chapter 1.3: Evaluating creativity   36
Chapter1.4: Seeking opportunities, designing and making   47

Section Two: Culture and cultural contexts for design and technology

Chapter 2.1: Children and cultural education   63
Chapter 2.2: The relationship between science and technology   73
Chapter 2.3: The relationship between design and technology and the arts   87
Chapter 2.4: Learning within and about different cultures and traditions   104

Section Three: Citizenship education through design and technology contexts

Chapter 3.1: Why citizenship?   125
Chapter 3.2: Becoming informed citizens through design and technology   138
Chapter 3.3: Developing skills for citizenship through design and technology   154
Chapter 3.4: Creating sustainable futures through participation   164

References   179

Index   185

Dedications:

AH – to Alison, Holly, Caleb and Hattie
DD – to Sally, Philip and Jacob
RR – to Jill, Anna, Kate and Lucy
for giving us the space and support to take risks and be creative

Notes on contributors

Alan Howe is Senior Lecturer in Primary Education at Bath Spa University College, where he has led and contributed to courses for teachers, undergraduates and postgraduates in design and technology, science and art and design. Prior to this post he taught in primary schools in Hertfordshire, Harrow, Bristol and Bath. He has recently managed a pilot project for the National Endowment for Science, Technology and the Arts aimed at stimulating children's creativity and innovation. He has a Biology degree and and an MA in Primary Education, the dissertation focusing on critical studies in primary art. This is his first book.

Dan Davies is currently Senior Lecturer in Primary Science and D&T Education at Bath Spa University College. He has a Physics degree and primary PGCE from the University of London, and has taught the full primary age range in South London schools. He worked for the Design Council as an education officer in the early 1990s, during which he initiated design and technology projects in primary schools across the south of England. He has an MA in Design and Technology Education, and has written his Ph.D. thesis on the relationship between science, design and technology in the minds and practice of primary student teachers.

Ron Ritchie is currently Associate Dean in the Faculty of Education at the University of the West of England. Whilst the book was being written he was Head of Department for Professional Development at Bath Spa University College where he was responsible for in-service education. He has been involved in the professional development of teachers in the area of design and technology for many years and has published widely in the field of primary education, including a successful book, *Primary Design and Technology: A Process for Learning'* (2nd edn 2001). David Fulton Publishers. He also co-wrote *Towards Effective Subject Leadership in the Primary School* with Derek Bell (1999, Open University Press).

Acknowledgements

The authors would like to thank:

Katherine Jarvis and children of Walcot Infants' School, Bath

Belinda Carter and Frances Hilton of The Garden Room Nursery, Bath

Alison Howe, the other staff and children of St. Philip's Primary School, Bath

Mandie Haywood, staff and children at Shawbury Primary School, Shrewsbury, Shropshire

Shoriza Clark, the other staff and children at Durand Primary School, South London

Sarah Jackson, Bev Ball, Judith Cock and the other staff and children of Christchurch Primary, Bradford-on-Avon, Wiltshire

Joanne Dent, Valerie Downes, Claire Garven and Hilary Pride of Horton Primary School, South Gloucestershire

Julia Sutcliffe, Sian Padgett, the other staff and children at Old Sodbury Primary School, South Gloucestershire

Richard White, Alison Ayres, the other staff and children at Bromley Heath Junior School, South Gloucestershire

Moira Hill, the other staff and children at Elm Park Primary School, Winterbourne, South Gloucestershire

Martin Palmer, the other staff and children at Ridge Junior School, Yate, South Gloucestershire

Jayne McCarthy, the other staff and children at Our Lady of Lourdes RC Primary School, Kingswood, Bristol.

Sarah Munday, the other staff and children at Bromley Heath Infants' School, South Gloucestershire

The staff and children of Chater Infants' School, Watford, Hertfordshire

The staff and children of St. James' CE Primary School, Bermondsey, Southwark

The staff and children of St. Lukes' CE Primary School, West Norwood, Lambeth

The staff and children of Newbridge St. John's Infants' School, Bath

Introduction

This is a book about primary design and technology, written for those concerned with the education of children aged 4–11: teachers, subject leaders, trainees, trainers, senior managers, advisors and governors. We will consider in some detail the current National Curriculum for England and Wales (DfEE/QCA 1999c), the National Scheme of Work for Design and Technology (QCA/DfEE 1998) and design and technology's relationship with the whole curriculum. But we do not begin in the primary classroom; we want firstly to address some much wider issues and raise some fundamental questions about the future. Rest assured, we will spend much of this book examining possible and practical approaches to teaching design and technology. We will illustrate these through reference to case studies set in primary schools.

We believe that design and technology has a great deal to offer the education of our young people, but that its full potential has yet to be realised. We claim here that design and technology can play a major role in the growth of young people and contribute to their ability to be active in the transformation of their society. These are high ideals, yet we hope this book will demonstrate that they are achievable, and that the work has already started. There are many traps waiting to catch us – few of the issues we raise are simple, straightforward or uncontested. We acknowledge this and will alert the reader to these debates where they arise. Those of you needing to dig deeper will be directed to sources of further reading. Ultimately we are concerned with offering the primary teacher ways forward from where we are now. But first, as our title states, this is a book about the future – but to which future and whose future do we refer?

We live in a developing country. The UK in the 21st century must develop if our children's children are to survive into the 22nd. There are increasingly clear signs that agricultural and industrial practices have led, and will continue to lead, to potentially devastating changes in our climate and our lives. It is said that the only thing predictable about the future is that it is unpredictable. We may not know which skills and knowledge will be required by children when they are adults, yet we do believe that we must teach children to understand the world as it is and to consider how they want their world to be. They must also learn to take action based on shared values in order to achieve a future that is sustainable. In order to do this they must approach the future creatively as members of a multicultural, multi-ethnic and democratic society.

They and we face, as ever, alternative futures. Since our technological development has given us a degree of control over our environment and other species, our future will be shared by the whole biosphere. One future might be a 'doomsday scenario' – our use of fossil fuels leads to climate change eventually making the planet uninhabitable. If this fails to materialise, there are other 'technological monsters' waiting in the wings to devour us – biotechnology, nuclear waste, ozone depletion, habitat degradation and so on. The failure of Western societies – particularly the USA – to implement the reductions in greenhouse gases agreed at the Rio and Kyoto summits makes this scenario seem increasingly likely. This is set against a backdrop of inequality in wealth between affluent countries of the 'north' and extreme poverty in the developing nations of the 'south' – racked by repeated viral and environmental catastrophes – which is clearly unsustainable over the coming decades, let alone the longer term.

Another possible future that is often portrayed is a sort of 'hi-tec utopia'. In this scenario, information technology succeeds in bringing us closer as a global community to solve the problems that confront us. In the recent White Paper on International Development it is claimed that: 'globalisation creates unprecedented new opportunities for sustainable development and poverty reduction' (Department for International Development (DFID) 2000: 12, para. 8). Rather than increasing inequality, the argument goes, the knowledge economy should be harnessed to create more open societies, where people have access to education and information that will help businesses in developing countries to compete globally. Rapid increases in prosperity through the integration of the global economy and the application of new technology should 'filter down' to the poor, assuming benevolent governments and transnational corporations. Unemployment in the north will be a thing of the past, with many bright young software engineers recruited from the south to plug the demographic gaps left by ageing populations. We may even be able to avert the environmental catastrophe by introducing more efficient technologies and reducing the need for travel.

Such optimism seems sorely misguided to many in the Green movement, for whom the assumption of continuous economic growth and technological development must be questioned, together with the real intentions of those wielding economic and political power. Orr (1993) demands that

> We must question the widespread assumption that our future is one of constantly evolving technology and that this is a good thing ... our imagination is increasingly confined to technological possibilities: faster and more powerful computers, television, virtual reality generators and genetic engineering.
>
> (1993: 18)

Thus the notion of 'sustainable development' takes on a more radical meaning – that the economies of the north must *contract* while the south pursues a different course, using indigenous and appropriate technologies that work in harmony with the biosphere.

> Students in the (21st century) will need to know how to create a civilisation that runs on sunlight, conserves energy, preserves biodiversity, protects soils and forests, develops sustainable local economies and restores the damage inflicted on the earth. In order to achieve such ecological education we need to transform our schools and universities.
>
> (1993: 16)

So what has all this to do with primary design and technology education? Everything. For whichever path we choose – or take by default through lack of will – a central determinant is our use of *technology*. We may anticipate a rather more mixed future than any of the above but we must acknowledge that ours is a technological society. We have to make a decision: do we control the development and use of technology, or are we controlled *by* it? The people who will make these choices in the *future* are in our primary schools now. In the UK, these children are following a curriculum which is largely rooted in the *past*. The debate during recent years over standards of reading, writing and arithmetic among primary-aged children has led to a narrowing, subject-bound curriculum that is dominated by literacy and numeracy, much as in the mid - 19th century. Onto this monolith have been 'bolted' some forward-looking themes, such as key skills, sustainability and citizenship, yet the area of the curriculum which can best claim to be *future-oriented* is design and technology. To test this claim, we need first to examine current practice.

Where are we now?

Following a period of turbulent change during the emergence of design and technology as a National Curriculum subject, the years since 1995 have seen a relative calm, which 'has led to a growing consensus as to the nature of design and technology and how it might be taught' (Barlex 2000: 5). In particular, the National Curriculum classification of design and technology into three types of activity – Investigating and Evaluation Activities (IEAs), Focused Practical Tasks (FPTs) and Design and Make Assignments (DMAs) – has clarified the requirements for many primary teachers (OFSTED 1998). The publication of a National Scheme of Work for Key Stages 1 and 2 (QCA/DfEE 1998) has further exemplified the approach, leading to widespread adoption by primary schools. There is evidence to suggest that teachers are allowing pupils more opportunities to take design decisions than in the early 1990s (OFSTED 1998, 1999a, 2001), although 'making' still predominates in many classrooms. Process-based models of design and technology activity are being used less prescriptively (Ritchie 2001), although the 'draw-before-you-make' mantra is still in widespread use.

In what we regard as best practice, children are involved in evaluating existing products, and are being given access to a wide range of resources to stimulate and develop ideas:

> They are guided to use interviews, questionnaires, books, magazines and information technology systems to find out more about the problem and potential solutions.
>
> (OFSTED 1999b: section 12.5)

The range of materials available for making has also expanded in many classrooms, although the 'technological use of resistant materials, paper and card has remained better than attainment with mouldable materials, textiles, food or electrical and mechanical components' (OFSTED 1999b: section 12.5). Children are becoming more familiar with the process of evaluating their own work, which informs teachers' assessment of the *procedural* aspects of design and technology practice (Kimbell *et al.* 1991). It is this notion of a 'process-based' subject that was so radical in 1990, and which enables children to 'image the future' by proposing and implementing changes to existing situations.

The *conceptual* aspects of design and technology (such as the understanding of structures and control systems) remain less well developed in the primary curriculum, leading to the removal of elements relating to structures from the 2000 Curriculum Order (DfEE/QCA 1999a). Associated with this area of design and technology *awareness* are those of *visual literacy* (e.g. Howe 1999 – see Chapter 1.3) and *technological literacy* (e.g. Siraj-Blatchford 1996 – see Chapter 3.2). The development of such areas of primary design and technology requires in our view a more cross-curricular approach than the narrow 'design and make' emphasis in much contemporary practice. Although there are indications that 'pupils make more use of what they have learned in other subjects and make better progress as a result' (OFSTED 1999b: section 12.5) design and technology has been increasingly taught in a single-subject mode in recent years. There have been signs that design and technology is being 'squeezed out' of the curriculum in many primary schools (Rogers and Davies 1999). While Curriculum 2000 offers an opportunity for the re-establishment of design and technology in primary schools, the progress that has been made in the last decade could be at risk unless we find new ways of arguing for its importance within children's wider education.

Why creativity, culture and citizenship?

Humankind has always faced a future that demands new and original thinking, innovation and invention. In the past we have responded with creativity. We must now prepare a new generation to respond in a similar way, even if the problems are of a very different nature to those faced by other generations. As we shall explore below, creativity is strongly related to a positive self-image. Primary schools are undoubtedly the place where self-image can be made or destroyed. We believe all children should emerge from their early years of schooling feeling positive about their own ability to contribute to our futures and empowered to do so. In order to make that contribution children must understand their own culture and the cultures of those they know and will meet. Of course it is essential that schools truly represent the cultural diversity that exists in our society in a way that leads to tolerance and understanding. In addition however, children need to think critically about the status quo and ask questions such as: 'Why are things as they are?' 'Who are the winners and who is paying the price?' 'Are there better ways of doing things?' It is only through understanding the cultural perspectives and values of others that these questions can be investigated. If children come to identify crises, injustices and inequalities without feeling empowered to do something, this can only lead to frustration, perhaps helplessness, even anger. This brings us to the book's third strand, that of citizenship. We shall interpret citizenship as an empowering concept, a way in which children can learn to become involved and knowledgeable about the processes of change within a democratic society. If design and technology is to be taught in such a way as to contribute to children's capability to participate in the challenges and dilemmas of the future then we believe the subject must embrace the three themes of creativity, cultural understanding and citizenship.

The structure of the rest of this book

We have introduced, albeit briefly, three key dimensions to the future of primary design and technology. As we proceed, these themes will be developed through critical engagement with debates. We will refer also to specific examples of primary design and technology teaching that exemplify these themes in practice. We have endeavoured to provide enough detail in the main case studies so that teachers might use them to inform their own planning and teaching. In some cases the teaching is clearly based on the National Scheme of Work for Design and Technology (DfEE/QCA 1998) and in all cases addresses the requirements of the programmes of study for design and technology in the National Curriculum for England (DfEE/QCA 1999a). We will show at every opportunity where strong links exist between design and technology and other subjects in the primary curriculum. We will also give detailed consideration to the important generic requirements of the National Curriculum – the 'Learning Across the Curriculum' section.

Section One: Creativity through design and technology for pupils and teachers

Chapter 1.1 begins by exploring creativity and the associated constructs of imagination and originality. We will examine the creative process and the place of creativity in education. Chapter 1.2 explores ways in which design and technology provides primary teachers with opportunities to teach for creative growth. We will consider the relationship between teaching for creativity and teaching creatively, together with the support required to sustain creativity. Chapter 1.3 looks at the central place evaluation has in design and technology and the creative process. Chapter 1.4 concludes the section by reviewing ways in which creative teachers can identify opportunities for teaching design and technology and how creative thinking skills can be developed.

Section Two: Culture and cultural contexts for design and technology

This section will explore the ways in which design and technology education can contribute to children's cultural awareness, understanding and apprenticeship. Chapter 2.1 provides a general introduction to issues related to cultural education and explores the way in which different cultural contexts can be used for design and technology activities in school. The rest of the section is structured around the three strands of cultural education identified in *All Our Futures* (National Advisory Committee on Creative and Cultural Education (NACCCE) 1999: 42): the cultural impact of science and technology (Chapter 2.2); the relationship between the arts, technology and design (Chapter 2.3); and finally, interaction between different cultural forms and traditions (Chapter 2.4). The last includes a discussion of multicultural and anti-racist approaches to design and technology education. In each strand, we will discuss teachers' creativity in identifying appropriate opportunities to enhance children's learning in design and technology, together with examples of children's creative response to those opportunities.

Section Three: Citizenship education through design and technology contexts

Chapter 3.1 asserts that design and technology shares many elements with citizen education, however it is conceived. We explore the model of citizenship offered in Curriculum 2000 and the levels at which children can begin to participate. In Chapter 3.2 we consider ways in which children can become 'informed' citizens, through understanding how products come to be as they are while questioning the direction of technological development. Chapter 3.3 considers how the skills of enquiry and communication that children develop through design and technology may be transferred to their citizenship education. Chapter 3.4 concludes the book by addressing the role of design and technology in active citizenship for a sustainable future.

Creativity through design and technology for pupils and teachers

What is creativity?

Purpose of this chapter

Through reading this chapter you will gain:

- an understanding of the ways in which creativity has been defined by others and our use of the term in the context of design and technology

- an understanding of the factors that influence creativity and creative growth.

Introduction

Creativity is an elusive, complex concept that is used in many ways in different contexts. Creativity is evident in all human endeavours; it is not exclusive to any one domain or discipline, although various groups would lead us to believe that it is. It has been variously described as an attribute; a process of, or ability in making connections; 'possibility thinking' (Craft 2000); a product of a process; a 'human resource' (Dust 1999); a characteristic of an activity (Yeomans 1996) or a form of learning (NACCCE 1999). There is an elitist definition of creativity that refers to achievements and innovations of the highest order. We might consider Leonardo da Vinci or Thomas Edison as examples of such creative genius. Research has shown (Dust 1999) that such achievers often have much in common – they have relatively little formal training in their field, or have rebelled against the training received and become obsessed and solitary people with little time for socialising. These 'geniuses' are, in fact, very few and far between. Those that are well known are also invariably from a

Western culture, white and male. It is exceedingly difficult to name world-renowned women or non-white inventors and technologists. Of course we refute the idea that the majority of humanity cannot be creative and not surprisingly, this book is founded on a somewhat more democratic definition.

NACCCE offers the following as a definition of creativity developed for educational contexts:

> Imaginative activity fashioned so as to produce outcomes that are both original and of value.

(NACCCE 1999: 29)

Unfortunately we cannot take the above at face value and proceed – each term within the definition can also be seen as contentious!

Imagination

Play is a vital aspect of creativity, and of learning in general. Imagination is a process of mental play, of playing around with ideas, yet it is also a mode of thought that goes beyond fantasising or recalling. It is the process of generating original thought and, in so doing, going beyond the 'conventional agreed' (Craft 2000; NACCCE 1999). It will often involve the making of connections between previously unconnected ideas.

A creative individual, Craft (2000) argues, must be aware of the unconventionality of his or her actions to be deemed 'imaginative'. If one is unaware of convention, as when a very young child draws the grass blue and the sky yellow, then this action or thought is not, strictly speaking, imaginative (although the way in which marks are used by the child to represent grass or trees or whatever may indeed be imaginative). If, on the other hand, a child knows that the convention of his/her peers is that grass is drawn green and the sky blue but *chooses* to do things differently, then imagination is at work. So creativity also involves 'the agent being aware of the unconventionality of what they are doing/thinking' (Craft 2000: 4). Craft uses the term *non-conventionality* to describe the above. We would prefer the term *post-conventionality* because it recognises that conventions are understood, but the creative individual has chosen to go beyond them, although not so far as to move out of the domain concerned. A creative architect might design a house incorporating huge innovation, but it still has to keep the rain off. It is at the boundaries of disciplines that creativity causes controversy. Sometimes the boundaries have to be shifted in order to accommodate the creative genius.

Originality

Can we expect children to produce something that is original every time they engage in a design and technology activity? Perhaps not, but to consider the *degree* to which an outcome is original is useful in an educational context. NACCCE have distinguished between three types of originality (1999: 30):

- To the individual
- Relative (to the peer group or cohort)
- Historic – i.e. unique

Is reinventing the wheel creative? It is if you have never seen a wheel before. Creativity is an ability and a willingness to *produce* something that is new to the individual. It is often the ability to make connections between previously unconnected ideas. Try these:

- Bricks and sculpture
- X-rays and medical diagnosis
- Multiple viewpoints and two-dimensional paintings
- Length of sides and angles of a triangle
- A ball and a wheel
- Clockwork and radio

The people that made connections between these ideas were uniquely creative. However, it is in the first and second sense of the above typology that children in school are likely to demonstrate originality.

Koestler identifies the paradox inherent in making connections:

> The creative act is not an act of creation in the sense of the Old Testament. It does not create something out of nothing; it uncovers, selects, re-shuffles, combines, synthesises, already existing facts, ideas, faculties, skills. The more familiar the parts, the more striking the whole.
>
> (Ashcroft and James 1999: 120)

It might otherwise be regarded as the 'Why didn't I think of that?' factor.

Value

The last part of our definition requires a judgement about value. But who is to say whether an outcome is of value or not? In the 'creativity literature' (Csikszentmihalyi 1990) the term *gatekeepers* is used to denote those members of a field that make judgements about whether an idea or outcome can be regarded as worthy. Art critics would be co-gatekeepers or members of the field within the fine art domain, or a research and development manager might be the gatekeeper of the domain of domestic appliance engineering. Gatekeepers are in a powerful position and have developed a broadly shared set of values – although of course they will often agree to disagree. We shall see later that the ideal in educational situations is for the judgements to be agreed upon through negotiation between the gatekeepers and those being judged; in school this will be teachers and, perhaps, children's peers, making judgements about children's work based on shared values. Furthermore, judgements about creativity in an educational context must operate on three levels. First there is the consideration *of the creative value* of the outcome, secondly the *effectiveness of the process*, and thirdly the *educational value* of the process and outcome. Each will be informed by beliefs and values held by the pupil and the teacher. Beliefs and values are therefore crucial to creativity and will be considered again in Chapter 1.3 and throughout Section Two of this book.

To summarise, we will proceed with caution using the NACCCE definition. Originality, imagination and values are the key components of creativity.

The creative process

There is a body of research that has sought to break down the creative process into stages (Dust 1999). A number of models have been proposed, identifying typically between four and seven distinct phases. We shall consider the four key phases common to many theories, namely preparation, incubation, illumination and verification. During the *preparation* phase a problem or opportunity is identified, information is gathered and ways forward envisaged. An example might be the long and detailed research phase undertaken by James Dyson before developing a novel approach to domestic vacuum cleaner design. *Incubation* is typified as an unconscious or subconscious phase, perhaps including time away from the task during which other, perhaps unrelated tasks are undertaken. The mind is still aware of the problem and will seek to connect day-to-day events with it. Maybe you can recall your mind flicking back at an unexpected moment, current events shedding new light on a problem or concern. *Illumination* occurs 'in a flash' when a key insight enables us to make that creative leap. This moment of creation occurred when the chemist Mendeleyev suddenly, after fitful sleep, saw the key pattern that enabled him to construct the periodic table of elements. This is not to say that we just have to sit back and wait for an idea to come to us; the preparation phase may be as arduous as the illumination phase is brief. *Verification* is the testing of the outcome, usually done through communicating to peers or gatekeepers in the domain. It is true to say that those most successful in their domain are able to convince the gatekeepers of the worth of their work. Those unable to do this, perhaps because they do not have access to the gatekeepers, or those that lack the persistence, will not succeed.

The above research derives from an elitist definition of creativity and does not shed light on how an individual might embark upon the process and learn the skills associated with creativity, or how the process might be supported. These are of course key questions for teachers. As we will see below, the place of the adult, as facilitator, permission-giver or mentor, is crucial throughout as is the environment and resources.

Education and creative growth

James (in Ashcroft and James 1999) refers to two types of creativity in educational contexts – *experiential creativity* and *professional creativity*. The former refers to the nurturing of creativity in learners and is what much of this section of the book is about. It is introduced in the next chapter as 'teaching for creativity'. Equally important, professional creativity refers to the idea of being creative as a teacher and is discussed towards the end of Chapter 1.2.

Creativity is an aspect of children's learning that has always been recognised as important by primary teachers in the UK, but the recent emphasis on the basics has meant teaching for creativity has become undervalued and, in some cases, neglected. 'Our society has not valued creativity (the present primary school curriculum is a good example of this)' (Dust 1999: 21).

A timely renewal of interest in developing children's creativity within primary education was heralded by the publication of the government-sponsored report *All Our Futures* from NACCCE (1999). The fact that a National Advisory Committee on the subject was set up itself indicates concern at the highest level. It is perhaps worth considering that it was the concerns of primary teachers' professional discourse referred to by Woods (1996) as 'fighting talk', voiced at innumerable meetings and conferences, that put creativity back on the agenda. If we look elsewhere in society, creativity is valued immensely. Industry and commerce crave it. Within the UK the creative industries (film-making, architecture, graphic design, fashion design, food technology, interior and landscape design, advertising etc.) and their associated entrepreneurial and retail activities are hugely important economically. People love to be creative in their leisure time. One only has to look through the TV schedules to identify two of the UK population's favourite pastimes – working with sheet/resistant materials and food – since DIY and cooking programmes abound!

If conditions are all wrong, creativity will simply not occur. Perhaps, in some situations, the fittest will survive – those robust and resilient individuals will struggle and strive to be creative. Research into factors associated with genius (*Guardian* 17 April 2000) found that remarkably creative individuals possessed extraordinary powers of concentration, perseverance and focus. Although some people manage to be hugely creative in spite of social, political or educational systems, there is no evidence to suggest that the best climate for nurturing creativity is one of adversity. There is no telling how many people have a potential to be creative which dies because it is not nurtured. If, however, optimal conditions for creative growth can be identified and maintained in schools, creativity will perhaps flourish in all its forms.

What are the right conditions for creative growth? Harrington (1990) brings the factors of process, people and physical environment together within a theoretical framework of the 'Creative Ecosystem'. He uses the biological ecosystem as an analogy. Just as a balanced ecosystem can sustain life, so a creative ecosystem could be said to sustain creative output. The attributes of the individual, the relationship between the individual and members of the system (peers/mentors) and the physical factors (resources and facilities, even comfortable circumstances) will all contribute to the likelihood of creativity flourishing. It is not only the environment (resources and spaces) but also the other members of the population (adults and peers) which will determine whether a child's creativity will blossom or wither.

Adults can have a key role in children's developing creativity (Dust 1999; Selwood *et al.* 1995; Woods 1996). Adults can perform a number of roles, including those of supporter, permission-giver, mentor or role model. It is also important to note how powerful an effect negative criticism can have on emerging self-image. Many of us can remember damning comments from adults that have stayed with us for life. Labels stick. A child labelled by a teacher as 'not-creative' is likely to live up to the expectation.

Can we teach children to be creative? Can we claim that schooling makes a difference? If so, we might hope to witness creative thought and action in school on a regular basis. How can we reconcile this with the idea that creativity produces the unexpected? Schools do have rules and constraints. Teachers are accountable. Is there a possibility for creativity within the rules? Imaginative activity will need to occur in the 'space' between conforming to and breaking the rules. We shall see that creative teaching is a question of making that space as accessible as possible. Ways in which schools can provide creative ecosystems for maximising creative growth will be considered in detail in the next three chapters.

Summary

Creativity, we believe, is within the potential of us all – there is certainly no evidence to suggest otherwise. We have also seen that creativity is associated with making connections, and is more likely to happen in interdisciplinary or boundary breaking situations. It must be the role of education to nurture the potential in all children by providing the conditions for growth.

Teaching for creativity and teaching creatively

Purpose of this chapter

Through reading this chapter you will gain:

- an understanding of how design and technology can be taught in a way that maximises children's creative development

- an understanding of how all teachers have the potential to teach creatively given appropriate support and opportunity

- an understanding of the issues related to support for teachers in school and at a national level.

Introduction

The aim of this chapter is to locate creativity in the mainstream of primary education and critically to re-evaluate its contribution to learning and teaching in the context of design and technology.

Within the primary design and technology curriculum there is a great deal of potential for creative thought and action. Indeed, the paragraph that opens the programmes of study for design and technology states that through the subject:

> pupils learn to think and intervene creatively to improve the quality of life. The subject calls for pupils to become autonomous and creative problem solvers ...
>
> (DfEE/QCA 1999c: 15)

It is interesting to note that all but two of the 'importance' statements for subjects in the current National Curriculum for England claim to contribute to children's creativity, yet design and technology is the only one to mention it twice!

Design and technology was originally conceived as a subject that would develop children's creativity. In the original proposals for the subject in the National Curriculum, the National Curriculum Design and Technology Working Group (1988: para. 1.2) noted that it involves the development of design and technology capability 'to operate effectively and creatively in the made world'.

Lady Parkes, chair of the working group, assured the secretaries of state that the approach to design and technology advocated was one that was:

> Intended to prepare pupils to meet the needs of the 21st century: to stimulate originality, enterprise, practical capability and the adaptability needed to cope with a rapidly changing society.
>
> (National Curriculum Design and Technology
> Working Group 1988: vii)

Over the years this intention seemed to get lost. In 1992 Stewart R. Sutherland, chair of the group charged with reviewing the orders, had very different matters in mind:

> A greater emphasis is placed on quality rather than quantity ... on making a manageable range of high quality products.
>
> (Review Group for Design and Technology 1992: vi)

The report goes on to discuss the 'characteristics of design and technology in schools':

> Our proposals reflect the view that design and technology involves identifying, analysing and meeting human needs for products and control systems. It requires practical ability to apply knowledge and skills when designing and making good-quality products.
>
> (Review Group for Design and Technology 1992: 5)

A shift is apparent. At its conception, design and technology had a very broad aim, that of preparing children to be creative, adaptable and well prepared to cope with an ever-changing society. By 1992 that aim had become much narrower and focused upon production. Through the Dearing Review of 1992–93 (Dearing 1993), the concerns were related to clarity, manageability and flexibility of the curriculum, with little time to consider a rationale for the subject. The slimming down that resulted removed any consideration of how design and technology would contribute to the education of our young people in a wider sense and left us in danger of forgetting how it contributes to children's developing creativity. The Design and Technology Association (DATA) produced a leaflet during this period that attempted to remind us of why design and technology was included in the curriculum:

> Learning design and technology at school helps to prepare young people for living and working in a technological world … It stimulates both intellectual and creative abilities and develops personal qualities.
>
> (DATA n.d.)

Few of us working in and with schools at the time would claim that design and technology was always presented to learners with such intentions in mind. Fryer (1996) found that among teachers and lecturers surveyed there was 'a pervasive view that creativity is only relevant to the arts'. This misconception is reinforced in Foundation Stage documentation (QCA/DfEE 2000a), where the area of learning entitled 'knowledge and understanding of the world' is said to prepare children for later work in design and technology, among other subjects. Another area of learning, that of 'creative development', claims to prepare children for art, music, dance, role-play and imaginative play. This is unfortunate – at this early stage in children's education both they and practitioners are being given the clear message that design and technology-based activities are separate from creative ones. We shall see in our first case study (below) that in practice this need not be the case. However, Davies (2001) found that two-thirds of student teachers questioned considered design and technology to be a creative subject.

The current National Curriculum documentation has restated the key role design and technology has in educating our children to be prepared to participate in creative, adaptable and active ways. Our target should be that everyone involved in the education of young children not only perceives the subject as one which can stimulate creativity, but understands how it can be presented as such.

Teaching for creativity

First we will consider what is known about climates that will promote creative thought and action and how these relate to the primary classroom. Freeman (1998 cited in Dust (1999)) summarises the finding of research into essential precursors for 'high-level' creativity, which are:

- Motivation and encouragement
- Knowledge
- Opportunity
- Courage to be different
- Creative teaching style

Some of these are attributes that might be enhanced or developed through direct teaching, others are factors that can be provided by the teacher. We might say they are ways in which we can *teach for creativity*. Through analysis of case studies we will shed light on teaching for creativity in primary design and technology contexts. Let us consider the above precursors in turn.

Motivation and encouragement

The most important motivators of children are parents, peers and teachers. When surveying the views of over 700 young people, Harland *et al.* (1995) found that interaction with known adults was cited as the single most significant way children were 'turned on' to creative and imaginative activities. Most frequently these positive influences were family, friends and teachers. Inspirational figures are sometimes perceived as 'cool', 'wacky' or somewhat 'anarchic' by children. Some teachers seem to be able to combine such eccentricity with responsibility, but it must be the aim of all teachers to offer encouragement and support. Of course, as well as intervening to support learning, teachers also need to maintain order in the classroom. Woods (1996: 3) has found that 'the less heavy handed the control, the more creativity was left for teaching and learning'. A young designer setting up his studio in the back streets of London was asked what it was he remembered about his own education. Without need to ponder he recalled a particular teacher who was always supportive and positive: 'this teacher never said no, you can't do that ... it was always yes – let's try it'. This suggests that it is a teacher's attitude, rather than personality, that may be the key. Attitudes such as curiosity, playfulness and open-mindedness are as vital in supporting adults as they are in children.

Research seems to indicate that intrinsic motivation (what we might call inner-drive and determination) is crucial to creativity. The research also suggests that extrinsic motivation, such as rewards, have a negative effect (Hennessey and Amibile (1988) cited in Dust 1999). The significance f the primary teacher is that s/he will need to carefully consider ways in which children are motivated to be engaged in design and technology. We are not advocating that children are just left to get on with being creative. Intervention will be required – perhaps to teach a skill, demonstrate a technique or sort out a problem. An essential skill of the teacher is to make the right intervention at the right time. We will need to look carefully at examples of classroom practice to identify the extent and nature of intervention in the creative classroom. The following case study shows the carefully considered ways in which one teacher chose to intervene.

Case Study 1 – Wheeled vehicles with a Reception class

Introduction
This first case study illustrates how the intrinsic motivation shown by a class of Reception children was identified by the class teacher and used as a starting point for design and technology activity. It goes on to explore the ways in which children's development towards the early learning goals can be encouraged through design and technology and other creative activities. The importance of play in designing and making is demonstrated very clearly. The case study also shows how in a Reception class, design and make assignments (DMAs) can fit within a holistic approach to creative development through skilful intervention.

Setting the scene
The Reception class at Walcot Infants' School, Bath, had lots of experience of working with a variety of construction kits on a small scale. There was a class craze for making ever-more elaborate wheeled vehicles. Katherine, the class teacher, wanted to capitalise and build on this enthusiasm. This led to her making formative assessments about what the children were able to do, their language development, their knowledge and understanding of the world and their interests. She had also identified a need to give the children opportunities to work on a larger scale and to develop the skills of cutting and joining wood.

The work was planned to encourage development towards a number of early learning goals, from the areas of language and literacy, knowledge and understanding of the world and creative development. Activities were planned and carried out over a period of two weeks.

The teaching sequence

To begin the project, Katherine discussed with the class their recently made wheeled models, and introduced a new word, 'axle'. She showed them how an axle could be used to link pairs of wheels and allow them to turn. Some children were able to make freehand labelled drawings of vehicles while others used the models as designs for the next stage.

The children were then given the opportunity to work with wood (balsa and other softwood) through structured play. The QCA/DfEE (2000a) *Curriculum Guidance for the Foundation Stage* recognises that 'children do not make a distinction between "play" and "work" and neither should practitioners'. The children discovered how PVA glue and elastic bands might be used to join pieces of wood through this activity. At times they became engrossed in this to such an extent that they lost all sense of time and place – they were 'in the flow', a feature of creativity.

Children responded to the task in very different ways; some made 'recognisable' objects while others explored the potential of the material by making 'assemblages'. Katherine introduced to them tools for cutting and shaping wood including a hand drill. There was much excitement at this stage and some children were interested initially only in cutting with the saws. It seemed crucial that this was allowed – the children were not interested in the task until they had fully explored the capability of the tools and learned to use them safely.

The motivation for the children to scale up their construction kit models was the opportunity to play with them after the kit models were broken up. The technique Katherine decided upon was one that might be seen as a transition between construction kits and working with resistant and recycled materials in that some of the components were provided, while some needed cutting and further shaping. Children made decisions about the number and size of components and the making began.

One child selected a ready-made stiff card axle support while another decided to use a drill to make two holes in a box (with adult help for measurement) and threaded through the dowel axle. One boy dismantled his first design of small wheels at the front and large 'tube wheels' at the rear because he found it didn't work – the body of the vehicle hit the ground. Two children noticed the card tubes and played with them. Here they discovered that they made a good 'telephone'. They also discovered that foam pipe lagging would slip over the tube. It was suggested that they might use this discovery to make a wheel and tyre. This pair continued to work very closely together throughout the making stage. Each learnt from the other, both making discoveries and innovating. They were careful to make their models identical – designing and making alongside each other.

After the first afternoon of making the class teacher encouraged an evaluation and sharing of progress. There was still a lot to do. Once the vehicle mechanisms were made, the basic structure was covered with paper and paste to provide additional strength and a blank surface on which to work. The introduction of paste and large brushes was another stimulus for some children to explore – one child played for some minutes with the paste, stirring it and calling it 'his porridge'. Eventually he had to be persuaded to remove his submerged arms from the paste to allow work to proceed. Another child was allowed to explore the paint and printing effect as a prelude to applying a finish. Again this play and exploration was supported, with intervention based on observation. The child's needs were put before the need to produce something. The class also had an opportunity to make images of wheeled vehicles using a block printing technique. There was further discussion about shapes combining to make the vehicle. Some children were given a further challenge – to make a door that opened and closed to let people into the vehicle. Outside in the playground the children had further experiences of wheels and axles through their play with bikes and trikes. The following week, when they were not being played with, the models were displayed in the class for parents and visitors to see. The children's interests had moved on.

Discussion

So what does the case study tell us about motivation and encouragement? First it would seem that finding out about children's interests and enthusiasms is vital if teaching is to be relevant and effective. There was a clear link in the case study between the children's interests and the subsequent planned activities. The integration of activities such as drawing, printing and outdoor play all served to preserve and perpetuate the initial enthusiasm. Once this rich vein of learning had been exploited then Katherine saw it was time to move on.

Secondly, the teacher was aware of striking a careful balance between encouragement, support and guidance. Play was encouraged and we have already seen how important playfulness is to creativity. Support was offered through the structuring of the task – the children could make decisions themselves while the choices offered all led to successful outcomes. Guidance built upon children's own discoveries, then at times new ideas, knowledge and techniques were introduced.

Another factor that the case study illustrates is that of providing space for creativity, both physically and in time. Children had the opportunity to work alone, in pairs or in groups. They were able to become independent by having easy access to resources and materials. The way in which the classroom was organised was therefore important. Space is important in another sense also – the space that a teacher allows for children to think and work things out for themselves.

> Too often we have a tendency to intervene earlier than we should ... early interventions often discourage rather than encourage.
>
> (Shallcross (1981) cited in Craft 2000: 14)

On several occasions, Katherine hesitated before intervening, preferring to let children follow through their own ideas, thus fostering autonomy.

Knowledge

Creativity in a given domain (discipline/subject area) is cultivated over time and depends on the individual having a very good grounding in the domain (Fleming's discovery of penicillin is an example of this). It must be the role of primary education to begin to provide that grounding in design and technology by introducing children to a range of materials, experiences, possible solutions and ways of working that will sustain them when meeting new challenges. Knowledge of materials, components and mechanisms is obviously required, but so is understanding of fields such as ergonomics (how products fit the dimensions of the human form) and aesthetics. A teacher's role will be to decide which knowledge would be useful for a child and to provide ways of introducing it in a relevant way. We shall see in Chapters 1.3 and 1.4 how evaluating the made world through Investigating and evaluation activities (IEAs) can provide knowledge that can be drawn upon in children's own making. Focused practical tasks (FPTs) are a second type of activity that will provide children with knowledge in a targeted way. Knowledge can also be derived from other areas of the curriculum – of materials from science, of decorative, finishing or drawing techniques from art, for example (see Section Two). The opportunities for children to gain such knowledge must be carefully planned. Children in the foundation stage will of course have relatively little knowledge and experience to draw upon. This short case study shows how at one nursery school careful planning ensures progressive development of relevant and linked knowledge.

Case Study 2 – Laying the foundations

Nursery school teachers Belinda and Frances describe below how they teach through an approach in which one topic runs into the next in a seasonal cycle because they recognise the importance of building upon knowledge and experience:

Early in the school year we asked our children to bring in an apple from home, or even one they had picked. This led to discussions about where the apple had come from, how they grew, the different types of apple, their colours and qualities, sizes, shapes, counting. The focus then turned to design and technology. Firstly, we made bakers' hats. This gave an opportunity to discuss hygiene matters and also made a link to the world of adult work. After much preparation and excitement, the children baked apple pies. Some were eaten shortly afterwards but most were packaged and sold to parents and carers. For some children the sequence was extended further as they wrote an 'apple pie book' in which they remembered and recorded the sequence of events.

Apples led to Harvest, Harvest to trees, trees to forests and Goldilocks, preparing the bear's house for Christmas. Our approach is for one thing to lead to another, topics unfolding, building experiences. The children would all know something; through touching, seeing, feeling, listening, to be used again.

As summer loomed day trips were planned, aeroplanes made and tickets sold. Passengers were shown to their correct seats as the pilot prepared for take-off. In Africa the children were able to use the binoculars they had made to look out for wild animals. By lunchtime the children were more than ready for the sandwiches they had made before they set out and carried in some very robust rucksacks that they had constructed earlier in the week.

Discussion

The case study shows how these teachers, recognising the importance of providing a sequence of experiences that would progressively allow children to gain knowledge in an experiential way, used a holistic approach. In their planning, the contribution of each area of learning was distinct yet they presented the activities in an integrated unfolding of the year's work. By doing so, they guaranteed that their young class, with a range of experiences and background, could participate fully in the creative activities planned.

Courage to be different

For children to be creative they will need to take risks. Risk-taking is an intrinsic part of creative behaviour. The downside to risk-taking is failure. In later life, the consequences of failure could be a low exam mark, a loss of a contract, even the loss of a job. Thankfully primary children are not usually under these pressures, yet failure will nonetheless seem real to them. We all know that children are very good at working out what it is the teacher wants. The messages, overt and implicit, that a teacher gives about what is acceptable and what is required, are therefore crucial. Another likely fear a child will have is that of ridicule by peers. For a teacher to give a child 'permission' to take risks and courage to be different, s/he must consider a number of contributory factors to the setting of a secure environment in which fear of failure is much reduced.

First, the classroom needs to be a safe haven. In all activities where children's work is very much on show – and there are few things more public than making in design and technology – a supportive environment is required. Children need to be trained in making positive and supportive comments about others' work. This ethos is unlikely to exist only during these activities, however; it will rely on the teacher providing times when all children's ideas, opinions and questions can be heard. It is likely that strategies such as circle time and positive approaches to behaviour management will be in place. There needs to be a 'can do' attitude prevalent in the class. The teacher must not perpetuate the expectation that some children are unlikely to succeed in design and technology, either explicitly or by not challenging children's self-perceptions. Within this culture of supportiveness and belonging, individuality can be nurtured and celebrated. If children see a teacher praising individual responses – a variety of ideas and originality – then others too will be encouraged. Some children will require a huge amount of reassurance. It is in this sense that differentiation by support is required. A good teacher will be able to make a significant difference to the number of children willing to have a go.

The following case study shows how children were given 'courage to be different' by the teacher.

Case Study 3 – Making sandwiches with Year 1

Introduction

This case study took place during one morning in a Year 1 class of 28 children at St. Philip's School in Bath. The children had very little prior experience of using food for design and technology. Many had never had the opportunity to make a sandwich before. Alison, the class teacher, although experienced, had little experience in teaching food technology. In response to these factors, she decided that the task would be simplified from the QCA/DfEE (1998) National Scheme of Work, Units 3B 'Sandwich snacks' and 1C 'Eat more fruit and vegetables'. Parents had been notified that the activity was due to take place and allergies and religious requirements catered for. There was a classroom helper at hand.

Setting the scene

The work took place towards the end of the autumn term and children had already engaged in two design and technology activities related to their theme of 'Parties' – designing and making party hats and invitations. During these activities, and in other contexts, the children had learned to trust their teacher Alison. They knew that their honest efforts would be valued and their successes celebrated. A positive and supportive ethos was prevalent in the class, where children felt valued and secure.

The teaching sequence

Alison began after morning registration by talking to the whole class on the carpet about sandwiches. Questions such as 'What is a sandwich?' 'How do you make a sandwich?' 'Which fillings and breads can go to make a sandwich?' 'Which sandwiches do you like?' led to some lively discussion. Alison used *Baked Beans, Bananas and Chocolate Sauce* by Susan McPadden and Neal Layton to widen children's ideas further. It was in a format similar to the books where children can 'mix or match' the head, body and legs of a character. In this case top, fillings and bottom could all be varied. It might have been worthwhile having some ready-made sandwiches to evaluate at this stage but budget and time did not allow for it.

The children were then asked to look at the ingredients provided – sliced white and wholemeal bread, finger rolls, chapattis, butter, margarine, Marmite, chocolate spread, jam, cress, bananas, cheese, ham and lettuce. They then sat for a few minutes and decided upon their design according to the ingredients available and an earlier discussion about the 'specification' for a sandwich and the 'criteria' set – that there should be due attention to health and safety matters and that they would enjoy eating it. As soon as they had made notes about their design and washed their hands they began making. The whole class made their sandwiches in the following 40 minutes. It was striking how much enthusiasm and concentration was evident among all the 5–6-year-olds and how their designs showed true originality. In discussion the children had listed a predictable range of fillings – jam, Marmite, chocolate spread and the like. Now in the class they were prepared to attempt such exotic combinations as cress and chocolate spread, ham and jam, banana and chocolate spread on chapatti. It might have been easy at this stage to question their choices – 'Are you sure you are going to eat that?' Alison, however, greeted each new and creative design positively and with enthusiasm. Evaluation of food technology is always popular (Figure 1.2.1) When the class had finished the children needed no encouragement to tuck in. With one exception (the child who had put every ingredient available into a chapatti) the children rated their creations highly.

Figure 1.2.1 Children evaluate their sandwiches

Discussion

The case study shows that all children can be creative given the opportunity and support. A positive teacher and a 'can do' atmosphere are required, but it cannot be switched on and off. Although teaching for creativity should occur across the curriculum, it can be at its most rewarding during design and technology activities. Is a teacher that teaches for creativity being creative herself? Does it matter if she considers herself non-creative? It is to these questions we now turn.

Creative teaching style

> Teaching for creativity involves teaching creatively ... to put it another way, teachers cannot develop the creative abilities of their pupils if their own creative abilities are suppressed.
>
> (NACCCE 1999: 90)

We conclude this chapter by claiming that *effective teaching must be our baseline yet creative teaching should be our goal.* Creative teachers provide vivid and motivational educational experiences of the highest order.

Creative teaching is a high-risk strategy requiring self-confidence and an investment of time and energy (Yeomans 1996). Creative teachers have been described as 'planning geniuses, innovators and experimenters' (Woods 1996: 10). Yet creative teaching is not chaotic. Paradoxically, children need clear structures otherwise they will not have the confidence to go beyond conventionality.

Teaching is certainly an activity that demands some creative solutions to the problems faced in every classroom every day. Halliwell (1993) assures us that creative teaching is not about being extraordinary, 'dazzling' or 'arty' but suggests that four qualities are required:

- A clear sense of need
- The ability to read the situation
- The willingness to take risks
- The ability to monitor and evaluate events

A sense of need derives from knowing the learner's needs, knowledge of the curriculum and subject. *The ability to read the situation* is about 'knowing what to do next' once the need has been identified and is again related to the curriculum, pedagogic knowledge and understanding of how children learn. The last point is very much a teaching skill. We shall dwell on *the willingness to take risks*. We have seen that risk-taking is an intrinsic part of creativity and requires attention to be paid to the support and ethos within the classroom. For teachers to take risks this support must be the responsibility of the school and even of our education system as a whole. School communities that are 'consciously creative' will have a better insight into the nature of creativity and better understand how they might provide for teachers and children to remain creative. There is a fine line between success and burnout. Colleagues, head teachers, local and national government all have a role to play in providing this support. There must be a culture of collaboration and of shared values for creative teaching to thrive.

The creative school

There are many aspects of teaching that depend on teamwork and the support of colleagues – to be creative in isolation is usually not sustainable. On the other hand, an alliance of just two colleagues can be a very powerful unit upon which great things can be built. A case study that illustrates this very well is that of the 'Shawbury Restaurant' project reported on the National Primary Trust website (www.rdiu.anglia.ac.uk/npt/). The report describes how one Year 5 class took on the considerable challenge of opening a restaurant for the night, inviting parents, friends and guests to dine from a menu prepared and served by the children themselves: a riskier enterprise is difficult to imagine! The class was fully involved in the organisational and preparation tasks, from advertising, taking telephone bookings, passing a Basic Food Hygiene test and developing a menu. The aims of the project were to inspire and enthuse a group of somewhat 'disinclined and disaffected' children, some of whom had special educational needs. A design and technology context was identified as a perfect vehicle to achieve these aims. In discussing the project, head teacher Mandie Haywood identifies a number of key elements associated with cooperation between colleagues that enabled the aims to be met. She writes:

> Class 5 needed revitalising and I knew that the restaurant project was the way to nourish them ... now all I required was another visionary with the confidence, practical creativity and stamina to put the concept into reality.

Fortunately, someone fitting the demanding job description was found – in fact a temporary teacher covering a maternity leave. Together the head, class teacher and children ensured the project was a great success, and that the aims were realised in subsequent weeks:

> It was a joy to see pupils working together, offering each other help in terms of support and tolerance, co-operating and celebrating each other's achievements.

> (Mandie Haywood)

An examination of the background to the project reveals that it was more than collaboration of the two colleagues that allowed risks to be taken and creative teaching to happen. There were discussions with the senior management team about how the work was to be integrated into the existing curriculum framework; parental support was crucial; local tradespeople, governors and friends of the school also contributed to its success. The message is clear: creative teaching is a whole-school issue. The more involved the school community becomes, the more rewarding the experience for all concerned.

Key players in developing the creative school are the head teacher and subject leaders. It is well established that the head teacher has a major influence on curriculum development in design and technology (Benson 2000). An unsupportive head teacher can contribute to the decay of the subject in a school. The Office for Standards in Education and Training (OFSTED) in its subject reports for 1999–2000 pulls no punches in this respect:

> D&T is at its weakest where senior managers do not understand the subject. For example, some schools have stopped teaching D&T altogether or only pay lipservice by the inclusion of one or two simple activities each year. These tend to be more 'craft' activity with a 'follow-my-leader' style of teaching that precludes pupils from thinking and designing for themselves, or even learning about materials and processes.
>
> (OFSTED 2001: 4)

Head teachers also have tremendous influence over the ethos and values of a school. The National Standards for Headteachers (Teacher Training Agency (TTA) 1998a) identify as a key aspect of headship, the requirement to 'provide inspiration and motivation' (1998a: 9). The subject leader or coordinator has similar responsibilities (TTA 1998b: 10) including a requirement to:

> Create a climate which enables other staff to develop and maintain positive attitudes towards the subject and confidence in teaching it.

With the head, subject leader and staff working together, motivational and inspirational teaching is possible. It is certainly a much easier proposition than a class teacher maintaining a creative teaching style alone.

It is during projects such as those to develop its buildings and grounds that the creative school is clearly seen at work. In Moorlands Infants' School in Bath, the challenge was to revamp the very large and high-ceilinged entrance hall and reception area, which doubled as a school fiction library. In this case, teachers, governors, parents and children combined with a TV production team to realise the aim of making the entrance hall welcoming and functional. In some ways the project was classic design and technology. There was an identification of needs involving all the users of the hall being canvassed as to their needs and opinions; a design phase in which a number of options were explored; evaluation of existing designs; a visit by children to a railway station to generate further ideas as a theme emerged; and then the realisation of the plans. By this stage the parents' association had managed to involve a TV company who were to do the work as part of a 'makeover' programme.

The making of the programme and the decoration of the hall were all completed in one hectic week, with a grand 'reveal' to the school on Friday. All involved in the project have very strong memories of the energy, excitement and positive atmosphere generated. It is at times like this that schools become the most fantastic places to work and study. The excitement dwindles as normality returns, yet the experiences gained have given both teachers and children confidence that such heights of creativity can be reached again. The children have moved on to the junior school, where they are about to embark upon a project to enliven their playground area. The infants' school has also turned its attention to developing the playground facilities. As a part of the QCA/DfEE (1998) unit of work on 'Playgrounds' (Unit 1B), the school has opened a discussion with children regarding the design of play equipment that will be constructed in their own playground. Work on the playground is underway outside as children carry out design and technology activities in the classroom. The children's work has a clear connection to a real context.

It might be argued that creative teaching is simply 'good teaching'. NACCCE (1999: 95) addresses this point and argues that creative teachers need more than the characteristics of 'good' teachers. Currently, definitions of *effective teaching* (OFSTED 2001) do not encompass notions of creativity. Effective teaching can be measured at a point in time, or perhaps determined through a performance over a year. The development of practitioners over a number of years must be sustained if, first, they are to remain motivated and effective and, secondly, they are to improve their practice. In order to improve, practitioners will need to risk experimentation, evaluate new ideas, imagine original ways of teaching – in short, to be creative. Ashcroft and James (1999: 25) warn that:

> Professional creativity should not be taken as suggesting some sort of runaway experimentation with what we do together. Rather, it asserts that responsible experimentation and innovation, planned and monitored with the help of colleagues as well as relevant theoretical notions, are desirable activities. Furthermore, they are the proper

concern of the professional teacher who wishes to keep the door open to improvement of their practice.

The case studies in this book show the creative teacher in action. Much of the teaching described is based on the National Scheme of Work (QCA/DfEE 1998), but with creative variations on the basic units of work. These examples show that this 'responsible experimentation' can result in innovative teaching that 'adds value' to children's educational experiences.

Kimbell (2000: 209) has shown, however, that the current educational climate appears not to encourage risk-taking or 'responsible experimentation' on the part of the teacher:

> Teachers know that naming and shaming is the order of the day. To hell with trust, faith and supportive risk taking environments.

He goes on to illustrate his point by sampling a number of OFSTED reports for their references to creativity.

> Of this total of 60,000 words, I invite the reader to speculate how many times the word 'creative' appears ... the answer is 1.
>
> (2000: 208)

He then informs us that the word 'manage' has a score of 87. He sums up the finding by concluding that:

> You might have the most tedious curriculum, but you had better be managing it well.
>
> (2000: 208)

The perception that exciting and demanding work is done in spite of, rather than because of the current climate in primary education is difficult to refute (NACCCE 1999: 8). Creative teachers, who in turn will be well placed to support and motivate creativity in children, will themselves flourish only with support, encouragement and opportunities for professional development. NACCCE (1999: 96) have recommended to the DfEE that:

> It is important to reduce or eliminate the factors which inhibit creative activity of teachers and learners ... There are risks here of de-skilling teachers and of encouraging conformity and passivity in some. At a national level we believe there are actions that the government should take to reduce these risks and promote higher levels of teacher autonomy and of creativity in teaching and learning.

At least one project has been set up to consider creative teaching in design and technology by the QCA and the Nuffield Foundation (www.nuffieldfoundation.org) which aims to provide 'national guidelines for developing creativity'.

Summary

We have seen how design and technology is a subject that can contribute greatly to children's creative development, yet in recent years this potential has not been fully recognised or realised. We have discussed ways in which teachers might facilitate creative thought and action through their teaching. We have recognised that all teachers have the potential to teach creatively given support and opportunity, and that creative teaching is more than 'merely' effective teaching. Creative teaching and learning cannot survive in isolation. Our schools and government have important roles to play.

CHAPTER 1.3

Evaluating creativity

Purpose of this chapter

Through reading this chapter you will gain:

- an understanding of the various ways in which evaluation occurs during design and technology

- an understanding of how evaluation can contribute to children's creative development

- an understanding of how evaluative thinking can be taught.

Introduction

Much of this book hinges on the premise that schooling can have a positive impact on children's creativity. If we can claim this strongly then it is more likely that teaching which develops children's creative potential will become an educational, social and political imperative. To establish that school makes a difference we might hope to witness creative thought and action in the classroom on a regular basis, yet how can we reconcile this with the idea that creativity produces the unexpected? The importance of *evaluation* in understanding children's learning and the roles of the teacher and child in this process need to be considered.

Our ultimate aim is for children to make a realistic self-evaluation of their creative output. Unless a child learns to 'stand outside' creative action, s/he is unlikely to achieve this goal (Sefton-Green and Sinker 2000). Those involved in creative domains will constantly make judgements about the worth of their efforts as well as seeking the evaluations of peers and the gatekeepers (see Chapter 1.1). We should begin to teach children critical thinking and evaluation skills, as indeed this is made explicit in the current National Curriculum for England (DfEE/QCA 1999c). Design and technology is, we suggest, an excellent context for the development of these skills.

Design and technology and evaluation have a special relationship. Evaluation is something that children *do* as an integral part of the subject. The ability to evaluate needs to be taught explicitly and is multifaceted. For the rest of this chapter, evaluation is taken here to mean the process of making judgements based on stated values. We recognise that children often perceive evaluation as the 'exercise of power carried out by schools over young people' (Sefton-Green and Sinker 2000: 220) and it is possible for that power to be wielded in a way that is detrimental. Ways in which evaluation can be constructive are therefore sought.

Evaluation in design and technology has five main strands:

- The work of others
- The children's own outcomes
- The process of designing and making in the classroom
- The learning that occurred (intended and unintended) (assessment)
- The roles played by the adults and children involved.

Evaluation is thus undertaken *within* and *of* a social context. *Assessment* is seen as a subset of evaluation. Assessment will be of children's learning – whether they have made progress against the learning objectives or intentions – by teachers or children themselves.

How do we teach children to evaluate? Before we go any further we must acknowledge that teaching children to evaluate is not an easy task.

> Evaluation as practised is always much more crude than theorists, even those grounded in practice, want to acknowledge. By definition, what happens in the day-to-day hurly burly cannot be as subtle as we would like.
>
> (Sefton-Green and Sinker 2000: 220)

Progression in evaluation

The teacher's work begins in the Foundation Stage (QCA/DfEE 2000a) where relevant early learning goals require children 'to use talk to organise, sequence and clarify thinking, ideas, feelings and events' which is summarised as 'language for thinking' (QCA/DfEE 2000a: 59) and 'responding to experiences, and expressing and communicating ideas' (QCA/DfEE 2000a: 127). Here we hit a problem. Design and technology is often perceived as, in essence, a practical subject. Evaluating is very much about thinking and articulating those thoughts, and as such is very dependent on language. We do not want to lose sight of the fact that design and technology is essentially 'the interaction of hand and mind' (Kimbell *et al.* 1991). To paraphrase Gardner's (1990) comments on similar issues in art education, it would be a tragedy if the subject became yet another venue for verbally talented children to 'show their stuff' while ceasing to provide opportunities for children to exercise physical, visual and spatial abilities.

As so often in education it is a question of striking a balance – in this case between the practical, active aspects of design and technology and those that involve reflection and discussion. We want children to be able to make evaluations and have confidence in the judgements they make, defending them if necessary. To achieve this they will need support and opportunities to develop these skills. In the early years, the emphasis should be on first-order ways of knowing – experience and action. Evaluation will begin with recall and *description*. By asking children to talk about what they have done, remembering the sequence of events and incidents along the way, the process will have begun. Most teachers have had the experience of asking young children questions such as 'can you think of ways of improving your model?' and getting a firm 'no' in reply. Young children find it notoriously difficult to make such comments; they do not have a conception that what they have done may in some way be inadequate and it is unfortunate if we plant the idea that this is the case. Sooner rather than later children will begin to be less than satisfied with the outcomes they produce. Why is this so? Need it be thus? It is well documented in art education that children will become much more critical and dissatisfied with their artwork as they reach a stage of development known as 'the gang-stage' or 'dawning realism' (Lowenfeld and Britten 1975). This coincides with children becoming more aware of themselves and others, especially peers, around the age of 8–9. Although we are not aware of similar extensive research in the area of design and technology, we surmise from our experience that it is around this age that children become more critical of their own outcomes. Allied to this increasingly self-critical streak in some children is a drop in self-esteem. There are two ways to look at these events: either they are developmentally inevitable, or they are as result of schooling and other life experiences. In either case, teachers need to take some action. If the former is the case then children will need all the support we can muster; if the latter is true then as teachers we must review the way in which children are taught to evaluate. As we have already seen, motivation and encouragement are vital to creativity. How do we ensure that evaluation is motivational and encouraging?

Developing criteria

The first 'rule' when evaluating is to be explicit about the *criteria* to be used. It is common practice in teaching to state clearly at the start of a lesson the learning objectives derived from curriculum requirements. Teachers will also make explicit their expectations about other aspects of classroom organisation and management, for example regarding behaviour, use of resources, group work etc. It is from a combination of these objectives and expectations that criteria for evaluating children's work can partly be drawn. A third source of criteria will come from a design brief and particular specifications associated with the DMA. Ideally these will have been developed through discussion and negotiation with the class. Once criteria have been established then it is important that they are revisited and that they are used. For example if our teaching objective was for children to learn

- 'to use existing fabric designs as inspiration for their own pattern-making'
- 'that some tasks have to be done prior to others' when involved in making 'Joseph's Coat' (QCA/DfEE 1998: Unit 2B)

and they were expected to access their own resources in a safe and cooperative way to make a coat with a specification that the coat would fit a 20cm doll, then the evaluation must be focused on these matters. Questions resulting from the activity might be:

- How does your design relate to the designs we looked at?
- Describe how you sequenced the tasks – did you do things in the best order?
- In what ways did you work safely?
- Did your coat fit the doll?

Through this we might avoid the intimidating and unproductive open question 'What can you do to improve this?'

If we are insufficiently clear about our criteria for evaluation at the outset, children are left to make their own minds up about what the teacher is looking for. Ollerenshaw and Ritchie (1997) found that in such situations pupils are liable to predict that aspects such as spelling and neatness are teachers' concerns. We know that it is not enough for teachers to respond to work with 'good', 'lovely' or 'could do better', yet in design and technology it can be all the harder for teachers to articulate their reasons for judgements. After all, how many of us *were taught* to make evaluative comments in our education, primary or otherwise?

Through engaging in the evaluation of ready-made products, children can develop the skills required to evaluate the work of others, and ultimately their own design and technology outcomes. The teacher too can develop these skills alongside the children. For this to begin there needs to be a regular opportunity for children to consider the made and the visual in a structured way and to become familiar with different ways of looking and knowing. The design and technology curriculum provides excellent opportunities for this through 'investigating and evaluating a range of familiar products, thinking about how they work, how they are used and the views of the people who use them' (DfEE/QCA 1999c: 94). Other areas of the primary curriculum also provide such opportunities. In history, science, art, religious education and perhaps other subjects too, children will be handling artefacts and learning about them and from them (Durbin *et al.* 1990). The skills required to interrogate objects are in some ways analogous to interrogating text and can be termed *visual literacy* (Howe 1999; Raney 1999). In becoming visually literate children become aesthetically aware, discerning and think critically – essential parts of the creative process.

Visual literacy

Visual literacy is a term that has come from the world of art and design education, being closely associated with the notion of 'critical studies' – learning to understand the work of other artists. In Howe (1999) it is claimed that the term also has relevance for design and technology, since for children to be able to appreciate the intentions of the designer of a product is to take the first step towards designing their own versions. But what is visual literacy? Is it a means for National Curriculum foundation subjects to hop on the literacy bandwagon and claim a more central role in children's education? Does the use of the literacy metaphor actually mean anything? Karen Raney (1999: 41) questions the assumptions underlying the use of such a term: 'Coupling "visual" with "literacy" … introduces the metaphor of language, provoking debates about the value of linguistic metaphors for getting to grips with visual things'.

Indeed, design might be seen as a 'third' mode of symbolic communication alongside language and mathematics, justifying its role in the curriculum through its development of *non-verbal* thought and communication (Thomas and Carroll 1979). Perhaps using the word 'literacy' risks confusing different types of learning in the minds of teachers and children? Elliot Eisner (1989) offers us one way of understanding visual literacy by seeing the whole curriculum as composed of different 'forms of representation'. Just as we seek to offer children the means to understand the ways in which words and numbers are used, so we ought to give them the 'keys' to unlock the meanings of other forms:

> In our culture, words, numbers, movements, images and patterns of sound are forms through which meaning is represented. To read these forms requires an understanding of their rules, their contexts, and their syntactical structures.
>
> (Eisner 1989: 24)

This approach has been interpreted somewhat narrowly and the metaphor used too literally in some secondary art education which equates the vocabulary of images with the elements of dot, line, shape, direction, tone, colour etc., and the syntax with the rules by which these are combined to communicate messages. This reading should not be restricted to works of art however; the entire visual world around us including posters, signs, manufactured objects and the media provides the 'texts' for children to interpret. For Raney (1999) such an approach needs to include an understanding of the intentions of the designers and their clients. It becomes a high-level activity, and one that we might doubt that primary children could perform. Yet the evidence from the implementation of the National Literacy Strategy is that children are able to discuss the intentions of an author in quite sophisticated ways, so why not those of a designer?

Approaches to investigative and evaluative activities

Although the skills required to be visually literate are *cross-curricular*, approaches taken by subjects such as art and design, history and design and technology have been in some ways different. All rely on the skill of the teacher in their selection and application, and are based on open-ended questioning in order to facilitate careful observation and investigation leading to the gains in knowledge and understanding through engagement with the visual world. A prerequisite of all is the ability to draw on experiences of similar encounters with artefacts (Howe 1999). Within art education practitioners refer to 'critical studies' approaches (Taylor 1986) developed through nearly two decades of research and practice. Within other subjects there is a more practical approach such as English Heritage's publication *A Teacher's Guide to Learning from Objects* (Durbin *et al.* 1990). In design and technology contexts Ritchie (2001) provides a framework of questions for design and technology contexts with the following headings:

- Function
- Process of making
- Human factors (with values implicit)
- Aesthetics
- Future developments (including evaluation of design success)
- Future evaluations (and connections with own making)

A slightly different approach, apparent in DATA's *The D & T Primary Co-ordinator's File* (1996) and *Planning into Practice* (1998) can be summarised thus:

- Relate to children's experiences.
- Focus discussion of artefacts/collection

    on form related to function

    on variation of design solutions

    on application of technology.

- Encourage investigation of components, elements of system.
- Allow children to develop for criteria for own design.

All the approaches listed above identify that children will need to be supported in developing their evaluative skills by teachers taking the role of 'somewhat more sophisticated individuals' (Gardner 1990: 14).

> These kinds of critical dialogues will not emerge naturally or spontaneously: they need deliberate teacher intervention and support.
>
> (Garvey and Quinlan 2000: 59)

In design and technology contexts for this support can be offered through questioning which focuses the attention on key aspects of the artefact. The evaluation needs to begin with questions that encourage closer observation and initial investigation, such as:

- What shapes can you see?
- What materials have been used?
- How many pieces have been used in construction?
- What does it feel/taste/smell like?

Questions requiring non-verbal responses might be:

- Can you make measurements of the dimensions of the item?

- Can you draw a part of the object?

Ritchie (2001) suggests a number of such questions a teacher might use to spur critical thought:

- What need or want does this fulfil?

- How was the design developed?

- For whom was it designed?

- Does the design discriminate?

The values that have informed the item should be explored where possible with questions such as:

- What effect will it have on people's lives and relationships?

- What effect will it have on the environment?

- What might the user think is important about the design?

The evaluation might then lead on to considering what has been learnt that can be applied to a design brief. We can see here how evaluation can develop knowledge and generate ideas. This process can be summarised as a cycle (Figure1.3.1). If teachers and pupils develop the language of evaluation during IEAs, the cycle can be reapplied to the children's own work.

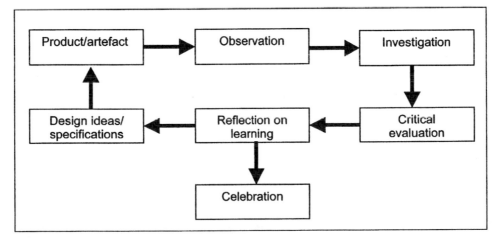

Figure 1.3.1 The evaluative cycle

As Figure 1.3.1 suggests, an additional aspect of evaluation when applied to children's work is that of *celebration*. Teachers have found many ways to mark the achievements of children. A recent innovation and a powerful tool for evaluation is the digital camera. The advantages of producing cheap and immediate images to display on screen or as hard copy are already apparent to many teachers, and seem to address two major design and technology problems. First, the storage and display of outcomes is often an issue as such displays are inevitably short term. Digital images can provide a lasting reminder of the achievements of the children and can also be used in record-keeping and reporting to parents. Secondly, it has been difficult to record, reflect upon and celebrate the *processes* of designing and making. Again, digital images can provide excellent material that can be used with a class to initiate discussion of what they have achieved and how they went about it.

A further way in which evaluation may be handled in a non-threatening way and without an implied deficit model is to ask the question 'what have we learnt?' When working with a Year 1 class on a sandwich-making assignment (see Chapter 1.2) Alison, the class teacher, got the following responses (Figure 1.3.2):

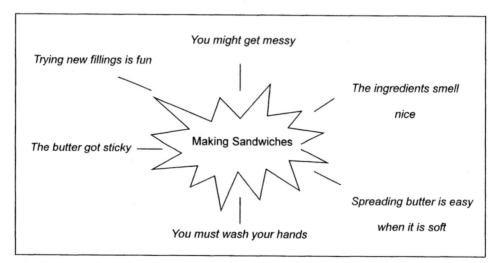

Figure 1.3.2 Learning outcomes – making sandwiches

Using this simple strategy to encourage reflection it is also possible to evaluate with the children the extent to which the teacher's objectives were met. This may also reveal unintended or unplanned-for outcomes. Here the comments suggest that the health and safety objectives were addressed and the children applied the skill of spreading butter. It also reveals that the children had enjoyed new experiences. Through such an approach, young children can be supported in reflecting on what has happened without the intimation that their product was in any way inferior. With older children, such a discussion can be part of a brief plenary where the stated criteria form

the agenda. Garvey and Quinlan (2000) offer other
strategies that are intended to support children in dev
skills.

Evaluating teaching

The creative teacher, as we have seen in Chapter 1.2, will be one who
concerned with his/her own professional development. A teacher who
wishes to evaluate the extent to which his/her teaching has encouraged
creativity might look for a number of indicators, discussed throughout this
section. By way of a summary, they are likely to include evidence of the
following:

- Opportunity for play and experimental activity.

- A non-threatening atmosphere in which children are secure enough to
  take risks and make mistakes.

- Opportunity for generative thought, where ideas are greeted openly
  (see Chapter 1.4).

- Time used in a way that acknowledges the creative process – e.g. time
  away from a task or problem.

- Opportunity for critical evaluation in a supportive environment.

- Children who have a sense of engagement and ownership of the ideas
  and tasks.

- Genuine opportunity for children to make decisions for themselves.

- Respect for the creativity of others.

- A sense of fulfilment and satisfaction for pupils and teachers
  concerned.

A teacher seeking to evaluate the extent to which s/he is teaching *for*
creativity is likely to obtain evidence of the above from a number of sources
– from observing the children at work, talking to and listening to them and
talking to others who know them. Additional sources will include
documentation and the observations of subject leaders and senior managers
made during their monitoring role.

Guidance is offered to OFSTED inspectors (also available to the class
teacher, published in *Inspecting Subjects 3–11* and available from OFSTED
www.ofsted.gov.uk). The publication provides a list of questions that might be
used by a class teacher, subject leader or anyone charged with the duty of

monitoring design and technology in school. Among the more predictable questions related to teaching, the question 'Is creativity fostered?' is included. It would seem that the question would need unpacking in a way we have tried to do above if it were to be answered in a comprehensive way.

The document also advises that:

> Pupils may be better at explaining their work orally than on paper. From discussion and the analysis of work judge if the work is challenging enough, and whether pupils are working to their potential. Listen to (children's) conversations, their questions and answers. Are they open to suggestions, willing to make changes and take risks as the work progresses?

The tone of the document does not contradict the approach we advocate in this book.

Summary

We have shown that in design and technology, evaluation is an important dimension of teaching for creativity. Children can learn evaluative skills through applying them to the work of others. When applied to children's own processes and outcomes, evaluation must be approached in a way that highlights learning and achievement. Ultimately, evaluation should lead to a celebration of success and progress if it is going to contribute to children's creativity. We have identified a number of criteria that a creative teacher might wish to use in order to make evaluative judgements about the extent to which teaching for creativity has occurred.

Seeking opportunities, designing and making

Purpose of this chapter

Through reading this chapter you will gain:

- an understanding of how a creative teacher can identify motivational and stimulating contexts for design and technology
- an understanding of the ways in which creative thinking can be taught
- an understanding of the ways in which teachers can support the development of initial ideas into readiness for making.

Introduction

We shall begin this chapter by considering the ways in which teachers can involve children in design and technology from the outset by identifying contexts and opportunities that motivate and stimulate creativity. We will then go on to explore the variety of methods applicable to the primary classroom that can be used to aid the generation and development of ideas – the essence of the designing phase in design and technology. Having good ideas is fundamental to creativity. This is an obvious point to make but do we actually teach children in a way that develops their ability to think creatively? The DfEE, on their website (www.dfee.gov.uk/a-z/creativityinschools.html) have suggested that there should be an 'increased emphasis' on thinking skills and creativity:

This will contribute to developing young people's capacity for original ideas ... for pupils to think flexibly and make reasoned judgements, they must be taught how to do it ... There are a number of different approaches schools might adopt to teach thinking skills: a general structured programme, targeting them within specific subjects, or infusing them across the curriculum.

We will address this targeted approach below. By new ideas we refer here not only to inventing new products but also to considering new ways of looking at things and doing things. We have already seen in Chapter 1.3 how the investigation and evaluation of existing products can stimulate children's ideas. There are also a number of other techniques that can be used to good effect with primary-age children to generate ideas to address needs, wants and problems. It is important to note that we are using 'ideas' in the plural here. We want children to be able to come up with a *number* of possibilities, *then* evaluate the potential before proceeding. We want to avoid situations where children say 'I can't think of anything' or on the other hand proceed with the first idea that occurred to them. This is not to say that every time children are involved with design and technology they should come up with three ideas and choose the best one – that would be too formulaic. We do believe children should have the opportunity to think before proceeding.

Seeking opportunities

In the original National Curriculum for Design and Technology (Department of Education and Science (DES)/Welsh Office (WO) 1990) it was required that pupils should be taught to identify needs and opportunities for design and technology. In practice, this proved very difficult for young children with limited experience of design and technology and left teachers wondering whether they were doing the right thing if they played too direct a role in this process. We have now come to understand that children do need support in this area, and that teachers will have to set up certain constraints and boundaries if the breadth and balance of experiences are to be maintained. On the other hand, children will respond more positively to design and technology if it seems relevant and worthwhile. Frost (1997) typifies creative teachers as 'writers of plays, creators of suspense, purveyors of novelty'. While writing their plans teachers do indeed compose a play in which the children will take a lead role. Teachers and pupils must therefore seek opportunities together for design and technology activity.

We feel there are three aspects to providing motivational and inspirational starting points for design and technology: identifying *children's interests*, *real opportunities* and *relevant contexts*. Maximising these aspects will lead to enhanced quality of engagement and outcomes. In Case Study 1 (Chapter 1.2) we saw how the class teacher used the children's interest to identify a context for learning. Section Two of this book discusses at length the importance of recognising the cultures in which children live and learn. In Case Study 8 (Chapter 2.4) we shall see how a teacher uses a story about his own travels to interest the children; in Case Study 9 (Chapter 2.4) a topical news story provides a context for learning. In Case Study 13 (Chapter 3.4) the children's home area is used to create a background to the work, and elsewhere in Chapter 3.4 the context of children's local environment provides opportunities for designing and making. In other examples, contexts are provided through the use of story or by referring to needs within the school – to help someone, to put on a play or to create a restaurant to entertain and feed others. In all these cases the teachers involved have shown how good quality teaching is enhanced by imaginative contexts for learning. Once the context has been identified, there will be considerable potential for the children themselves to identify particular opportunities for designing and making.

Seeding generative thinking

The mind, once stretched, never goes back to its original dimensions
Wendel (cited in Fisher 1998)

Before we look at some techniques for generating and developing ideas we need to consider the ideal conditions or contexts for thinking new thoughts. Claxton (1998) uses the analogy of gestation to explore these conditions. The analogy requires a creator (mother) and a seed or germ of an idea. If the idea is to grow it needs to be nurtured and provided with the right conditions.

The seed will not germinate unless it makes contact with a body of knowledge ... The evidence from studies of conspicuous innovators suggests that this pre-existing body is most fecund when it is full of rich experience.

(Claxton 1998: 71)

In translating this analogy for design and technology, where does the seed come from and what are the right conditions? As we have seen in Case Study 2, the foundation stage has a role in providing rich experience, while in

Chapter 1.3 evaluating the work of others was recognised as a starting point for design and technology. Through investigative and evaluative activities children begin to develop their own body of knowledge about needs and wants, products, materials and techniques. In this way the teacher can begin to offer the rich experience children will draw upon when designing themselves. Richness infers variety. Teachers will need to plan for a variety of experiences of encounters with a range of products with different uses, from different cultures, from different times and places (see Section Two).

Encounters with designers and technologists

Children's experience, and hence the resources on which they can draw for designing and making, can be enriched through visits to stimulating or unusual exhibitions, buildings or environments. Experience can also be enhanced through meeting people who have needs and wants different to children's own – older people, children from other places and adults working in a range of industries. These encounters need not all take place within design and technology contexts, yet all will serve to increase the richness of children's experience and hence their ability to be creative. But the most important kinds of encounters for stimulating creativity are those involving practising designers, technologists, artists, architects and engineers – we will call them 'design-related professionals'.

One of the key findings from research into children's creativity is the central importance relationships have in the creative process (Harland *et al.* 1995; Selwood *et al.* 1995; Sharp and Dust 1997). Time and again research in the field points to the vital role peers, supportive adults and role models have in inspiring and stimulating children. Most of the literature in this area is related to the arts rather than design and technology. The concept of the artist in residence is well established and the benefits for children are widely recognised. It is often the case that the artist will be working in a way that closely parallels a design process, i.e. there is likely to be a need or want identified, perhaps by a client; a generating ideas phase that may involve modelling or sketching; some form of making and a role for evaluation throughout the process.

Occasionally children have the opportunity to work with a different kind of design-related professional. For example, children in several Bristol primary schools have recently worked with architects from the city's architectural workshop to design 'homes for heroes'. Chater Infants' School in Watford (see Chapter 3.4) invited a furniture designer from the company who had designed their tables, chairs and storage units. The children interviewed him and then worked alongside him designing their own storage furniture. Francis O'Connor, a theatre set and costume designer, worked with Year 5 pupils at St. Luke's CE Primary School in Lambeth while they were producing a class opera (see Chapter 2.3). What can these kinds of experience offer to enhance children's creativity in designing and making?

Davies (1996) claims that young children have a natural affinity with designers since the ways in which they approach situations have certain common features. For example, designers often:

- explore designed objects through play as part of the process of generating ideas

- tell stories about the users of the products they are designing

- use knowledge from a wide variety of different sources in approaching design tasks

- make a conceptual leap into an idea ... before extensive analysis and synthesis of the problem.

(Davies 1996: 46)

When asked about why children responded to him in a different way to their usual classroom work, Francis O'Connor offered the following explanation:

Children have less fear of making mistakes than adults, as long as you don't constrain them to a small scale, which is inhibiting. I tend to work on a very large scale with children: huge sheets of brown paper in a big space, which is very liberating. You can't control it the way you can a pencil and rubber. It depends how children are led; if they are shown possibilities at the beginning it sometimes constrains their ideas, so I tend to wait until half way through before making suggestions ... I don't try to teach design – design happens in the head as well as in the hands. You can be taught skills and methods, but designing is instinctive. I can stimulate children to design, by talking with them, finding out what their ideas are, what the piece is about. This is the most important stage. Sometimes when you're teaching, your own aesthetic and history informs, but also constrains the pupils. At a young age, children have an aesthetic informed by their own perspective, through their own eyes. Later they understand through other people. I try to take them back to when they weren't constrained – working on a big scale in a big space.

(Davies 1996: 49)

Our experiences of working with children and designers together are that they are able to talk the same language, and build on the approaches they have in common. Children respond instinctively to the apprenticeship model of education offered by the designer in the classroom, rather than to the more rigid, curriculum-led attempts to teach children to design. Children need the opportunity to refine and integrate their intrinsic design skills and understanding, through engaging in real design projects with real designers. Such experiences can provide opportunities to:

- develop positive relationships with adults other than parents and teachers
- gain insights into the professional design world – the nature and processes of designing and making
- understand artistic processes – how artists gain inspiration, the importance of research, experimentation and progress.

If there is an opportunity to work with the designer then the child will:

- try new approaches – experiment and take risks
- develop new skills
- develop new knowledge – about traditions, techniques and materials
- develop enthusiasm, enjoyment and confidence.

Unfortunately, it would seem that this kind of experience is rarely offered to children. NACCCE (1999: 126) reports that 'developing creative partnerships does not yet have high enough priority in many schools'. The report goes on to cite a survey that found in a five-month period:

- 50% of children had not been to a play
- 80% had not been to a museum, gallery or concert
- 90% had not been to a dance or opera
- 97% of children who had been to an event enjoyed it.

What is striking about this snapshot, apart from the impoverished nature of the education some children are offered, is that the research does not consider encounters with designer-related professionals. Is it because they are not seen as creative partnerships or that the researchers forgot to ask? Either way, this can be taken as indicative of the distance we have to go before such enriching experiences become a part of an educational norm, and as such provides a significant challenge for the curriculum developers of design and technology in the coming years. On a note of optimism, the National Endowment for Science, Technology and the Arts (www.nesta.org.uk) has just commissioned a pilot project to promote encounters between children and design-related professionals in order to stimulate children's creativity and innovation.

Generating ideas

The human brain is very good at organising ideas and information. We have an inherent sense of classifying, sorting and pattern-seeking. When we see stars in the sky or points on a page we cannot accept that they are randomly scattered. We have an innate desire to see images, figures and faces that assure us there is pattern and order in our world. This attribute is very important to us, yet it can also inhibit creativity. It is sometimes difficult to see things in new ways; to rearrange the information we have to create new patterns or associations. Chow, cited in Claxton (1998), speculates that:

> seeing through an existing, invisible assumption, which is often the key to creativity, requires a mind that is informed but not deformed; channelled but not rutted.

> (Claxton 1998: 72)

Such an informed mind might be termed as having a 'creative disposition' (Fisher 1998). Such a disposition is guided by the question 'What other ideas are there?'

How do we develop a mind with a creative disposition? Many people claim that thinking skills are not automatic, but can be developed. Indeed McGuiness (1999) cites no less than six recent major approaches to teaching thinking skills directly. Most examples are related to science, history, geography, moral and philosophical contexts. None, however, claim to address creative thinking skills in design and technology contexts.

De Bono (1970) coined the phrase 'lateral thinking' to describe the process of *generative* thinking and contrasts it with 'vertical thinking' which is typified by being *selective*: a step-by-step process where at each stage a logical way forward is selected. Lateral thinking, on the other hand, provokes the brain into creating new patterns and insights. 'Rightness is what matters in vertical thinking. Richness is what matters in lateral thinking' (de Bono 1970: 37).

De Bono goes on to describe how lateral thinking will explore unlikely ways forward. This generative thinking is a prelude to designing, and as such should not be aimed at finding the best or most reasonable or likely alternative. Its purpose is to provide different approaches. A favourite example comes from a National Curriculum Council (NCC) in-service training pack (1991). A scenario is provided: a class of children run in from playtime and one of them trips over a coat left on the floor and bangs their nose. We are asked to generate a number of possible ways to avoid another accident. Try it before proceeding and jot down your ideas, no matter how odd.

When giving this task to any group of pupils, students or teachers, a number of suggestions will be made: redesign coat hooks (use Velcro/bigger hooks); encourage children to behave more carefully (have rules/monitors/signs); remove the need for coats (ban coats/provide umbrellas) or ensure if an accident happens it will be not be serious (padded floor/nose guards for all).

It is a temptation to evaluate ideas immediately – 'surely parents wouldn't agree to a ban on coats', 'a nose guard is just silly!' – yet this instant response can be counter-productive. In some cases the participants will giggle at seemingly silly suggestions, so it is only the brave that will speak out. For those that find creative thinking hard, any negative peer pressure, no matter how subtle, will provide an excuse to stop thinking. Being creative, as we have seen, is a risky business – there will always be a percentage of those unwilling to risk being laughed at or thought of as daft. The teacher's role is to reduce that percentage as much as possible by encouraging a supportive and open ethos in the classroom.

The above is an example of possibly the most common way of generating ideas, sometimes called *Brainstorming or Blue-sky thinking*. Essentially this is an uninterrupted process during which we avoid evaluating the ideas immediately, and certainly do not laugh at them!

Linking thinking

Linking ideas, as we have seen, is a fundamental part of creativity. There are a number of techniques that can help this linking thinking. Relating a product in an analogous way can throw up new possibilities. For example, *Packages are like*

... nuts (strong, keep the contents safe, hard to open)

... homes (keep contents dry, secure, insulated, reflect the owner's character).

Develop the analogy for the item to be packaged. *If my new sweet was growing on a tree, it would look like this ... be displayed like this ... be dispersed like this ... be consumed by* and so on. Random links and associations can also help. For example:

Modes of transport and ... (dip into a dictionary or the nearest piece of writing). What associated ideas emerge? *Vehicles and ... dolphin – streamlined, grey, intelligent, waterproof ... banana – yellow, bent, open by unzipping ...*

Visual and auditory triggers

Some children might find the visual a more powerful stimulation than words. Visual triggers might come from:

- random shapes/scribbles/doodles
- images from photos or clippings
- digital photos manipulated
- shapes in nature – fruits, river deltas, frost patterns.

They might be asked to collect clippings from magazines to relate to their design focusing on, for example:

- the user
- product form, shape, texture, colour or pattern
- places where the product will be used.

Listening to music could also stimulate some children. What kind of moving toy, fairground ride or monster does the music suggest?

Role play

In generating ideas, children might be asked to act out an aspect of the life of the intended user or even the intended product. Some adult designers have actually done this, e.g. dressing like a pregnant woman or visually impaired person. One designer, Patricia Moore, spent three years travelling as an 85-year-old with a costume that restricted her movement, hearing and vision (Design Council 2001). Examples for role play could include:

- looking after a baby
- coping in a classroom without bending
- if I were a package I would be …
- a day in the life of a slipper.

Group discussion

Generating ideas need not be done individually – we can all recall images of designers bouncing ideas around. This may be something of a cliché yet generating ideas as a group has distinct advantages. The discussion may start from a very open-ended question such as 'what winds you up?' or completing the statement 'we really must do something about …'.

There is certainly no need in primary design and technology contexts for children to work alone in the initial stages of designing. If children work together they can spark off each other, thus enriching the experience rather than limiting it. We may be concerned that children will copy someone else's idea. If this happens it may indicate that not enough time was given to the idea generation phase or the child did not receive enough support. It is wrong to suppose that they *could not* think of an idea, just that they did not *appear* to. Buzan and Buzan (1993) have suggested that there will be surprisingly few common ideas among a group of like-minded people. They found that in simple word association exercises, most words generated were *unique* to one individual.

> The human brain can make an infinite number of associations; and our creative thinking is similarly infinite … every human being is far more individual and unique than has hitherto been surmised.
>
> (Buzan and Buzan 1993: 68)

The implications for classroom practice are clear – each child will have the potential to offer a new insight or idea that can be pooled and they are therefore a valuable part of the process. The teacher's role here is to set up group situations in which such potential can be realised, and children can learn to feel positive about their ability to contribute to a class effort.

Developing ideas

A second aspect to generative thinking is playing around with ideas. During this process ideas can be developed or perhaps new ideas may emerge. Good designers are people that have not lost the ability to play. Claxton (1998) describes some work by Getzels and Csikszentmihalyi who investigated how art students worked on a task of composing a still life. The research concluded that the most original outcomes were produced by students who had played more with the objects, and who 'delayed foreclosing on the picture as long as possible, changing their minds as they went along' (Claxton 1998: 83). By play in the above context we mean handling objects and exploring them in a relatively unstructured way. In a primary classroom children might be encouraged to handle objects such as the materials they will later be using (see Case Study 1, Chapter 1.2). This will help children to develop their knowledge of the properties of materials and will also allow them to image how the materials might be put to use. They may use materials that allow shapes and forms to be developed in a temporary way.

- Clay – on deciding a form for a storage container/candle holder/vehicle superstructure.

- Pipe-cleaners or art straws – to allow exploration of stable shapes for a photo frame (QCA/DfEE 1998 Unit 3D)/furniture/playground equipment.

- Paper – to allow exploration of card mechanisms, patterns for garments, patterns for bags or shoes.

- Construction kits – to allow exploration of mechanisms for vehicles or toys, hinges for storage boxes, stable shapes, strong shapes.

Younger children are likely to require considerably more support than older ones in developing their ideas. Siraj-Blatchford (1996) illustrates how this might be done by providing children with a 'highly scaffolded' task (referring to Bruner's ideas about supporting learners) in which children made up a provided net for a model litter bin. Along the way the class learned about two-dimensional nets for three-dimensional objects, cutting, folding and scoring as they all succeeded in making the model. The key to the success of this structured approach in terms of allowing creativity was that the process did not stop at this point. The making of the model was, in essence, an FPT which then led, via an evaluation of the litter bin, to a DMA undertaken by groups of children when they were asked to improve upon what proved to be (intentionally) a rather inadequate teacher's design. This approach also has connections with the evaluation of existing designs (Chapter 1.3) but in this case the children have learned some skills as they made up the model. Siraj-Blatchford refers to a progression from *collective design* – working as a group with support from the teacher – to a *design collective* in later years in which children draw on earlier experiences and learned skills to design and make with autonomy alongside their peers. If children are part of successful design collectives during the early years, where appropriate teaching which supports them ensures success, then they are more likely to progress to more challenging tasks with confidence.

Further thoughts

It is evident that in order to think, one needs time. All that has been described so far is time-consuming. The idea of keeping open options for as long as possible and not making up one's mind seems an anathema to current imperatives for pace and progress. There is, however, a wealth of evidence to suggest that when people are faced with pressures of time they tend to revert to linear, conventional, less creative ways of thinking.

Traditional methods of communicating design are based on talking, drawing and writing and these still have an important place in primary design and technology. However, the power of information communications and technology (ICT) in inspiring and supporting creativity has yet to be fully realised. There is potential in the areas of digital image, the Internet as a research tool, and computer-aided design (CAD). Specialised software (such as TABS+ Aspex) allows children to make three-dimensional models and print out two-dimensional nets. 'My World' allows children to make a number of decisions, for example in relation to designing a house; it is particularly appropriate for early years settings.

Making

The structure of this chapter may have implied a rather linear model for designing, from identifying needs, through generating and developing ideas to making. Design and technology has always suffered from the need to describe it as a process, which often results in a model that in essence is sequential. Others have described a zigzagging interaction of hand and mind (Kimbell *et al.* 1991) or a spiralling or circular process (Siraj-Blatchford 1996). These sophisticated models attempt to make the point that design and technology teaching is rarely an ordered affair in the classroom, not least because children do not learn in a neat sequential way. Making is a 'hands-on' and also a 'minds-on' activity.

We do not want to pretend that if the above advice has been followed then during the next lesson the children will all be ready for an uninterrupted bout of making. We have discussed creative and generative thinking as a part of designing, yet there is more thinking, and drawing upon knowledge, to be done when making. At any point, the introduction of one of the strategies we have described might refresh or refocus minds. The teacher will need to consider the nature and level of intervention required to support children as they make – it is in this way differentiation will occur. We have seen that creativity is associated with knowledge. Through making with a range of materials, children will develop knowledge of materials which in turn can be applied to further making. There is no substitute for this first-hand experience. From it children will also learn skills of cutting, fixing, joining and manipulating that will enable them to realise their creativity. Making artefacts and products therefore becomes both a way of learning and an outcome of learning. All of the full case studies and many other examples of practice cited in this book refer to children making using a range of materials available in primary schools –

construction kits, textiles, food, resistant materials, card, paper, electrical and mechanical components. In each case there are subtle differences apparent between starting points, ideas generation, support strategies, FPTs and evaluative activities. Within the classrooms where these case studies occurred there will have been even more subtle differences about how each child went about the task of designing and making. We have not reported the countless incidents of evaluative discussions with peers and teacher, innumerable steps back and learning immediately applied to the problem faced, repeated examples of original thinking emerging from the mêlée of activity around the classroom table. We ask the reader to proceed with caution – we will leave some of the details to your imagination.

Creativity and culture

We have considered ways in which design and technology can contribute to creative development, yet creativity cannot occur in a cultural vacuum. We have seen that culture and subculture determines whether creativity is valued. Culture provides the context for creative activity. Creative activity can bring about an understanding of culture and an appreciation of the creativity of others. It is to these matters that we turn in Section Two.

Summary

Having ideas is a fundamental aspect of designing, yet children will not be motivated to think if the tasks seem irrelevant or uninspiring. Design and technology has a great deal to offer towards the development of generative thinking skills. We have reviewed a number of techniques and approaches to generating and developing ideas. Generative thinking must be founded on rich and varied experiences and encounters. Once ideas have been generated, attention must turn to the support that teachers can give to the development of initial ideas.

To return to the research of Getzels and Csikszentmihalyi (in Claxton 1998), a follow-up survey, seven years later, found the most successful students (in terms of being successful practising creative professionals) were those that had maintained a playful and patient way of working. Seven years is the time most children spend in our primary schools. Is it too idealistic to hope that future generations of children will be leaving Key Stage 2 with a playful and patient approach to learning?

Culture and cultural contexts for design and technology

Children and cultural education

Purpose of this chapter

Through reading this chapter you will gain:

- an understanding of the broad way in which the term 'culture' is being used in this book
- an understanding of the different cultural contexts children experience and their relationship with design and technology education.

Introduction

This section will explore the multiple roles of culture within design and technology education. It will build on the ideas about creativity introduced in Section One and show their relationship to design and technology activities focused on particular cultural contexts.

Children learn from experience, but not from experience alone; this experience is usually gained in a social context. It is well recognised that this interaction with others affects children's learning. Less often emphasised is that learning takes place within specific cultural contexts. If this is recognised by teachers, then subjects such as design and technology can provide them with opportunities for developing children's cultural awareness and understanding of their place in the world. As part of this cultural context, this section will explore the relationship between design and technology and other aspects of the curriculum.

It could be argued that children should be taught in a way that minimises the impact of the cultural context. Indeed, the French philosopher Rousseau (1712–1778), who was an early advocate of learning by experience, took this view. In his book about the education of a boy called Emile (Rousseau 1911) he allowed the child only one book, *Robinson Crusoe*, which he described as 'the narrative of a man, shipwrecked and isolated from all others, having to build up a world cut off from his historic civilisation'. It was a book from which Emile could gain practical knowledge without being constrained by cultural influences. Rousseau regarded this as a 'paradise'. We do not agree, preferring the view of Pascall (1992: 1) who aspires 'not so much to free pupils from the manacles of culture, as to place the cultural dimension at the heart of education'. However our view of the cultural dimension is somewhat broader than Pascall's, embracing multiculturalism and a global perspective.

Culture is a contested and problematic concept that has many meanings. At this stage of our discussion, we are taking it to mean, very broadly, 'the shared values and patterns of behaviour that characterises different social groups and communities' (NACCCE 1999: 42).

This chapter begins with a general discussion about culture and children's experience of the cultures in which they live and learn. We will explore the multiple identities that children construct as they deal with and move through the complex mix of cultures within global, European, national and local communities. We will emphasise the significance of the values and beliefs underpinning these cultures, relating these to the values in design and technology education.

Cultures are dynamic, diverse, evolving and difficult to define. In this context the following themes (highlighted by NACCCE 1999: 42) need to be discussed in relation to design and technology education:

- the cultural impact of science and technology
- the relationship between the arts and technology and design
- the interaction between different cultural forms and traditions.

These themes will form the basis for the remainder of Section Two, but first we need to consider how children encounter the concept of culture.

Children and culture

We all experience a variety of different social situations in our lives which effectively involve us in different cultures: some to which we may feel that we belong, others with which we are associated to varying degrees and some in which we feel outsiders. Take a few minutes to reflect on the various identities you have (the different 'hats' you wear) associated with different settings in which you live and work – perhaps as offspring, parent, teacher, tennis player, football fan, worshipper, voluntary helper etc.

Similarly, children have direct and indirect experiences of global, European, national and local groups and communities. These differing groups and communities involve different cultures and related power structures. Such experiences help children to understand themselves and define their own identities. Before exploring some of these experiences, we should, of course, recognise that children's identities are strongly affected by factors such as gender, ethnicity, social class and physical characteristics (Siraj-Blatchford and MacLeod-Brudenell 1999: 36) which will influence and moderate the impact of children's experiences on their understanding. We will be referring to these important factors in later chapters.

Children sometimes write their own addresses in a way that reminds us of the levels of their understanding of themselves: *Me, My house, My road, My town, My county, My country, Europe, The World, The Universe.* We will limit ourselves to terrestrial ones at this stage of our discussion.

Children's immediate and direct social relationships will provide their most obvious cultural experiences. These will be associated with home, their extended family and friendship groups. Every family has its unique traditions, ways of doing things, values, power relationships and even language codes; in this way the child experiences what might be described as his/her home culture. As soon as a child starts school s/he is likely to have to deal with different cultures in the classroom, in the playground, as a member of a sports team or school club. Different power relationships become apparent and the child's understanding of how the social world works becomes increasingly complex. The construction of their identities may also be influenced by local events such as carnivals, festivals or visits to places of worship. For example, a child of African-Caribbean origin attending a Caribbean-influenced carnival may have certain aspects of his/her sense of identity modified, enhanced or reinforced by the experience. The same child attending a Diwali celebration with a friend may construct, from that experience, a different understanding of his/her identity within a multicultural society. Children gain an awareness that some cultures are more dominant and/or more highly valued than others, and that tensions can exist within and between the different groups with whom they are involved.

Children also begin to form identities that have a regional or national dimension, but these will probably be more indirect. However, supporting the local or national football team may establish in the child an association with a different cultural group. Watching *Top of the Pops* or a TV soap, listening to Radio One or seeing a film that is featured in the media, joining in with the latest craze, sharing in the response to a national celebration (a Royal wedding) or tragedy (a rail crash) – all contribute in differing ways to the child's evolving understanding of their place in the world. More direct experiences, for example visits to relatives or friends in other parts of the country where accents and ways of doing things vary, add another layer to children's understanding of themselves and others.

Aspects of European and global identities may also evolve during childhood. For some children holidays on campsites in France, during which they meet and play with those from other European countries, can begin a process in which their understanding of being a European develops. This can be further developed through visitors they meet from other countries and links between European school partners. Children's European identities may be informed by emerging understanding of similarities between their lives and those of others, and the differences that they begin to identify and (ideally) respect. For others, watching European sports championships, song contests and other events may develop a different understanding of Europe and of being European. Clearly, the potential for such experiences to lead to negative and/or stereotypical views and attitudes exists alongside the positive.

At a global level, children's identities as members of an international community will most often evolve through indirect experiences. Consider the impact on children of the media coverage of the Millennium celebrations; the potential for these celebrations – despite reservations some may have had about them – to help children see themselves as citizens of the world was considerable. Events such as the Olympics or natural disasters also bring the global community together; children are increasingly exposed to these experiences indirectly through the media. This generation of children is also growing up in an age in which the Internet and other technologies allow them to communicate with others all over the world without difficulty. For them the global village will be a reality, and the friend that a child talks to about the latest boy or girl band may well be on the other side of the world. Of course, there are negative aspects to modern communications and the impact that images – such as those of apparently helpless populations during natural disasters in the economically less developed south – can have in reinforcing unhelpful stereotypes. At this level, the dominance of certain values and languages reminds us, again, of the complex and problematic nature of cultural education.

To return to a more positive theme, for those children in schools enriched by the diversity of pupils from many different ethnic groups (some of whom may be recent arrivals in the country) the experiences of a global dimension are direct and potentially more productive. We will return to this theme in Chapter 2.4.

All of the above experiences shape children as human beings. They provide the contexts in which they learn and through which they can be creative. Many of these experiences occur beyond school. However, it is our contention that teachers can make the links between them and school much stronger, particularly, we believe, through design and technology: reinforcing the relevance of school to everyday life and fostering children's awareness and understanding of the diverse groups and communities in which they live.

Culture in Curriculum 2000

Cultural education has always been a part of the thinking underpinning the National Curriculum. Two objectives of the 1988 Education Reform Act (DES/WO 1988) were to: 'promote the spiritual, moral, cultural, mental and physical development of pupils and of society' and to prepare them for 'the opportunities, responsibilities and experiences of adult life'. The Act was intended to provide a 'broad and balanced' education for all. The extent to which these aims have been realised is debatable and the danger inherent in the Act being seen to promote one cultural viewpoint as superior to others needs challenging. However, the latest incarnation of the National Curriculum emphasises the importance of cultural education and citizenship much more than its predecessors (DfEE/QCA 1999c). It also promotes a view of cultural development which is broader than that included in the original Act:

> The school curriculum ... should develop [children's] knowledge, understanding and appreciation of their own and different beliefs and cultures, and how these influence individuals and society.
>
> (DfEE/QCA 1999c: 11)

In the design and technology curriculum (DfEE/QCA 1999a), we read that design and technology contributes to cultural understanding:

> through explaining the contribution of products to the quality of life within different cultures and through valuing and reflecting on the responses of people from other cultures to design solutions.
>
> (DfEE/QCA 1999a: 8)

This seems somewhat at odds with the all-encompassing generic statement above. We believe that design and technology can contribute to cultural understanding in a much broader way than merely through looking at the 'contribution of products' and 'design solutions' to cultures. Looking at products is a start, but design and technology can also provide a number of opportunities to engage children in culturally based activities. Schooling should also provide children with the cultural awareness and understanding that they will need if they are to make informed choices to enrich their lives and contribute to the development of the society in which they live. This involves the *values* dimension of the curriculum, to which we now turn.

The place of values in education

Values are derived from the beliefs an individual holds about the nature of people and things: such as 'all individuals should be respected' or 'recyclable materials should be used whenever possible'. Different groups and communities will hold a range of differing values and belief systems between which children move and within which they can clarify and develop their own unique values and beliefs. These will include areas such as human nature; environmental factors; ethnicity; social matters; relationships with other communities; religion and economics – all of which are of importance to design and technology.

Reflect, for a few minutes, on the values involved in two contrasting cultural settings for children: the school football team and a place of worship. Children learn to move from one setting to another, often very quickly but not always easily. Trouble can obviously occur when things get muddled; the values of the playground and the language associated with them get used inadvertently in the classroom. For this reason, children need to be supported in understanding their values, their origins and their impact on others in different situations.

The question of values that might define the 'English' (Paxman 1998) is receiving attention within the current debate about nationality and devolution in the UK. It is, in our view, unhelpful to try to identify core values that are unique to any specific community or culture. Cultures are more complex and diverse than this, having evolved over time and resulted from constant cross-fertilisation. That does not mean that schools cannot identify and foster consensus values such as compassion, kindness and justice to underpin the formal curriculum, as well as others, identified by the school as valid in the particular context in which they are promoted. Indeed, Curriculum 2000 makes explicit values such as these, which are said to underpin it. The document claims that 'schools and teachers can have confidence that there is general agreement in society upon these values.

They can therefore expect the support and encouragement of society if they base their teaching and the school ethos on these values' (DfEE/QCA 1999c: 147).

The statement of values in the National Curriculum covers *self*, *relationships, society and the environment*. Under *self*, the statement is: 'We value ourselves as unique human beings capable of spiritual, moral, intellectual and physical growth and development'. There are statements related to this such as: 'We should make responsible use of our talents, rights and opportunities', which are relevant to our current discussion. Under *relationships* we find the following: 'We value others for themselves, not only for what they have or what they can do for us. We value relationships as fundamental to the development and fulfilment of ourselves and others, and to the good of the community'. This is amplified with references to respecting and valuing others as well as working cooperatively. Under *society*: 'We value truth, freedom, justice, human rights, the rule of law and collective effort for the common good. In particular, we value families as sources of love and support for all their members, and as the basis of a society in which people care for others'. Supporting statements cover: understanding and carrying out our responsibilities as citizens; refusing to support values or actions that may be harmful to individuals or communities; respecting religious and cultural diversity. The problematic nature of some of these statements now becomes evident. For example, can we expect pupils to accept and 'own' values about families that do not correspond to their own experiences of family life? Such statements should not be adopted uncritically by teachers. Values related to the environment include: accepting responsibility for maintaining a sustainable environment; ensuring that development can be justified; and repairing, wherever possible, habitats damaged by human development and other means. Chapter 3.4 includes examples of work related to environmental concerns. Design and technology offers particular potential for enabling children to address values included in the National Curriculum statement as we now explore.

Values and design and technology

Values play a vital part in design and technology education (Layton 1992; Ritchie 2001). Because, as we have argued above, design and technology in school and the wider community always takes place within a cultural context, those involved will inevitably operate within particular value systems that affect behaviours and decisions. Children can begin to be made aware of these value systems and recognise their significance. So what values might be involved in design and technology? A product may embody a belief about individual freedom or maximising happiness; it may be informed by using limited resources with care or not wasting other people's time, or even a preference for a particular colour or shape. Decisions taken during designing and making are inevitably value-laden, and children need to be made aware of the implication of their own values and those of others whose needs they might be considering. The constraints involved in a particular project often mean that the outcome created is not congruent with the values of the creator. For example, the designer of a car – whose values might include the belief that cars should be as safe as possible – may reduce safety features because of constraints on the selling price.

In the classroom, very young children's values in design and technology may be restricted to personal likes and dislikes. As teachers we need to help them recognise the basis for preferences expressed in order to help them become more open-minded. They should be made aware of the preferences of others and recognise they may be different to their own. Older children can be invited to deal with more sophisticated questions that involve value judgements concerned with economic, aesthetic, environmental, technical or social issues (Benson 1992). For example, a problem regarding too much litter in a school playground could be solved by designing and making litter bins or educating others not to drop litter. The decision is a value-laden one that requires children to consider their own and other people's attitudes.

Introduction to other chapters in Section Two

The remainder of this chapter introduces the three themes that set the agenda for the rest of this section. They are, we believe, areas in which links between culture and design and technology are of greatest significance.

The cultural impact of science and technology (Chapter 2.2)

Science and technology have transformed human perceptions of how the world works and our roles in it. They have directly changed the practical circumstances of our everyday lives; it has been argued that science was the dominant culture of the 20th century and is set to become even more dominant in the 21st. However, this is by no means unproblematic; no one would argue that the results of science and technology have always had a positive impact. The key question is: how can we, through design and technology education, increase children's awareness of this and allow them to interact effectively with the made world?

Technologies can have devastating effects on people and the environment. Recent years have seen an increasing awareness in society at large of some of the implications of technological developments. However, much remains to be done to educate future citizens to ensure they remain vigilant to the excesses of technology and those who engage in it. Whether the issue is global pollution or the impact of genetic engineering, if individuals are to make decisions about issues like these, through the ballot box or in other ways, they need to be well informed and able to deal with conflicting evidence and opinions. Teachers have a responsibility to ensure schools play a part in ensuring children are educated with an awareness and understanding to play a full part as future citizens and members of their local, national and international communities.

The relationship between the arts and design and technology (Chapter 2.3)

We believe that it is time for the relationship between the arts and technology to be re-evaluated in a more positive and constructive manner. The role of creativity in both areas is one way to bridge the divide. Chapter 2.3 will explore the relationship between design and technology and other aspects of the school curriculum traditionally associated with the 'high' culture of art, music and drama. It will further explore the relationship between popular culture and arts that are traditionally associated with people who describe themselves as cultured. The ways in which children can be introduced to the arts, for example through images and artefacts, will be examined. The chapter will emphasise the importance of children being introduced to folk/traditional cultural experiences as well as considering the impact of new technologies on current cultural trends (e.g. music and other visual media).

The interaction between different cultural forms and traditions (Chapter 2.4)

Design and technology activities can be set in a range of different contexts that reflect the diverse cultural experiences of the children. Design and technology has the potential for raising children's awareness and understanding of other times and places. For example, children's understanding of technologies in other historical periods can impact on their understanding of their own culture and identity. Exploration of the ways in which people live in other places (for example, as a result of the climate or geographic factors) help children learn to value and respect diversity and to learn from others. Chapter 2.4 will address differences between multicultural approaches to design and technology and anti-racist approaches. This will emphasise the opportunities afforded by multicultural approaches (for example, evaluation of musical instruments or breads made by people from different cultures) to raise children's awareness and understanding of a pluralist society. Anti-racist approaches will provide examples of design and technology that more explicitly confront potentially racist attitudes and behaviours.

Summary

Both culture and values are challenging and multi-layered concepts. We have considered how culture relates to children's lives and their education, and explored values in education and, specifically, in design and technology contexts. We have introduced three key culture-related themes that are explored in the following chapters.

The relationship between science and technology

Purpose of this chapter

Through reading this chapter you will gain:

- an understanding of the significance of science and technology as a part of national culture

- an understanding of the different ways in which the relationship between science and technology can be viewed

- ideas about how these different views relate to approaches to teaching science and design and technology

- insights into the way that children can be made aware of the nature of science and technology and the implications of this for their lives.

Introduction

Professor Sir Harold Kroto (one of the UK's Nobel prize-winning scientists) is quoted in *All Our Futures* as saying that 'science is the dominant culture of the 20th century and is set to become even more dominant in the 21st' (NACCCE 1999: 43). Not all would go this far, but no one would deny that science and technology have an impact on our lives in the 21st century and that this is likely to increase. The nature of that impact is more contested – for some the transformation of daily lives through the use of technology is regarded positively, for others the adverse effects of technologies on people and the environment mean that technological progress is viewed in much more critical ways. Technology creates 'winners and losers' and can cause some to be 'dominated and disenfranchised by the dominant technological forms' (Siraj-Blatchford 1996: 9). This point is further developed in Chapter 3.2.

The significance of science and technology to our lives highlights the need to recognise the link between these endeavours and the cultures within which they develop. This is an iterative relationship: scientific and technological activities cannot be isolated from their cultural context. Cultures evolve in part because of the opportunities and threats that science and technology create. To understand culture in a society requires us to explore the role of science and technology in that society.

The relationship between science and technology is also complex and this chapter explores these links in the world beyond school and between the subjects of science and design and technology in the curriculum. We will stress the importance of children learning about the natures of science and technology and their impact on our lives. We will address the question of how, through design and technology education, we can increase children's awareness of these issues in order to help them to interact effectively and critically with the made world and in the society in which they are growing up.

There are significant similarities as well as differences between science and design and technology in schools. One of the similarities is that both provide opportunities for children to be creative (see Chapter 1.1). Indeed, success in both inevitably requires creativity, whether the context is school or the world beyond school. As the NACCCE report states:

> Science and technology offer profound evidence of the variety of human creativity and they are implicated at every level in the formation and expression of the social culture ... Any definition of cultural education must take account of this.
>
> (NACCCE 1999: 44)

Science and technology in the world beyond school

Let's begin with a difficult question: which came first, science or technology? This could be seen as a 'chicken and egg' question, although many would see technology as predating science since (as discussed further in Chapter 2.4) many societies were using technologies, such as levers and pulleys or navigation aids, before sophisticated explanations of how the technology worked were articulated. However, that is to oversimplify things; the relationship between science and technology in society has engaged the minds of philosophers and others since science, as we understand it, began. At its simplest, science can be seen as the pursuit of knowledge and understanding about the world around us, while technology can be seen as a means of changing the material conditions in which we live while drawing upon the knowledge of many domains. Design and technology, as defined in the National Curriculum, emphasises the processes by which tangible outcomes are produced to meet human needs or wants through the application of knowledge. However, Layton (1993) warns us against adopting such simplistic models. For much of the population, distinguishing science and technology might be regarded as unnecessary – the term 'science and technology' is regularly and unproblematically used to cover a wide range of human activities and outcomes. For those of us involved in education however, a clearer understanding of the relationship is required to enable us to teach a curriculum which includes two subjects – 'science' and 'design and technology' – in a coherent and appropriate way.

Gardner (1994) provides a more sophisticated model to help us see the relationship between science and technology in the world beyond school. He suggests that the two domains can be viewed in the following ways:

- as indistinguishable (the common sense view described above)

- as science preceding technology, or technology as applied science (TAS) (as immortalised in the Zanussi advertising slogan 'the appliance of science')

- as independent, with differing goals, methods and outcomes (a demarcationist view, illustrated by the simple distinction drawn above)

- as technology preceding science (a materialist view in which technology provides the tools – both physical and conceptual – for science)

- as interactionist – scientists and technologists learn from each other in mutually beneficial ways.

Davies (1997, 2001) provides a thorough discussion of these differing perspectives in the context of primary education. For the purposes of this book, we choose to adopt an *interactionist* model in order to identify the maximum benefits of learning in both subjects within the curriculum. However, the complexities of the debates can be shared with pupils. For example, Galileo's story could be used to illustrate the indistinguishable view – was he a technologist (designing and making telescopes) or a scientist (developing theories of planetary motion)? The same example could support a *materialist* view – that he needed the telescope in order to collect observations to develop his ideas. Solomon (1995) offers some helpful materials that provide stories from history to be used in teaching technology, which also have some clear scientific dimensions.

Having considered the relationship between science and technology, we should also acknowledge the complexity of the term 'design and technology'. This is not a term much used beyond schools and it blurs even further the relationship between science and technology by adding 'design' into the equation. Design and technology was conceived in its original form as a 'unitary concept, to be spoken in one breath as it were ... intended to emphasise the intimate connection between the two activities as well as to imply a concept which is broader than either design or technology individually and the whole of which we believe is educationally important' (National Curriculum Design and Technology Working Group 1988: 2). It combines the processes of generating, developing and communicating ideas with the creative application of knowledge, skills and understanding to design and make products. It is as simple and as complex as that! The term consequently ensures that the curriculum subject covers a broad range of media and contexts. It addresses activities that beyond school involve a spectrum of designers and makers including food technologists, architects, fashion designers, potters and furniture makers.

Before moving on to explore the relationship between science and design and technology in the primary school curriculum, it is worth reminding ourselves that design and technology has a link with all curriculum areas, not just science. The present discussion concentrates on the relationship with science because of the particular implications of this for pupils developing understanding of the cultural context of the 21st century.

Links between science and design and technology in the curriculum

The National Curriculum outlines what teachers have to teach; it does not specify in detail how the content should be taught (except, it could be argued, in the case of the literacy and numeracy strategies). Consequently, teachers – collectively as a whole-school staff or individually – are making professional decisions about how to teach science and design and technology and whether to link them. If we use Gardner's model (see above) we might see the two subjects taught in the following ways:

• As indistinguishable – for example, a cross-curricular thematic approach or project, such as one on 'Movement', in which no attempt is made to distinguish subject areas in the planning and implementation of activities. Another example could be an open-ended problem-solving approach that might draw on science or design and technology (without children being aware of the discipline in which they are working). There might be parallels here with the early learning goals approach to the Foundation Stage (QCA/DfEE 2000a) in which subject labels are not as important as the broader aspects of children's learning.

- As science preceding technology, or technology as applied science – for example, science lessons on simple electric circuits lead to a follow-up challenge in which the children are asked to make a working torch. There is some suggestion of this approach in the National Curriculum statement of 'The Importance of Science' (DfEE/QCA 1999c: 76, quoted below).

- As independent – science and design and technology taught as completely distinct and unrelated lessons. For example, science lessons in a particular week might cover simple electric circuits while the design and technology lessons might focus on evaluating musical instruments with no link intended.

- As technology preceding science – pupils are challenged to design and make something and when the need for an investigation or scientific knowledge arises it leads to appropriate scientific activities. For example, designing and making model bridges might raise questions about the strength of different shaped girders. This could lead to a separate but related follow-up activity investigating the strength of girders.

- As interactionist – learning in both subjects results from a close but appropriate linking between activities. For example, children trying to design and make a raincoat for teddy will be expected to carry out an investigation into which fabrics are waterproof, not simply to choose the best for the raincoat but also to increase their understanding of the properties of materials.

Each of these approaches, with perhaps the exception of the third (independent), have potential for fostering children's understanding of the relationship between science and design and technology as part of their development of cultural understanding. The interactionist approach, however, is likely to provide the broadest understanding of the way in which the two subjects contribute to and gain from each other, benefiting learning in both subjects as well as contributing to children's understanding of their contribution to cultures.

Jarvis and Rennie (2000) provide guidance on eliciting children's ideas about technology and give evidence of the common ideas they hold (for example technology being associated with 'high' technology and modern electrical or electronic products). They offer strategies for extending children's ideas where necessary to give them a broader, more representative view. One of our aims would be to encourage children to recognise the equal importance of design and technology alongside science – the interactionist approach that we are advocating is one way of ensuring a balance is achieved. That balance also needs to be achieved in terms of children recognising the benefits that can result from both areas alongside a critical awareness of the threats and concerns that may be involved.

The teacher's choice about the approach to adopt can be seen as an aspect of creative teaching; identifying ways in which the subjects can be taught in a balanced way that values each and fosters learning in each. Additionally, focusing on links between the two areas can lead to efficient use of curriculum time; most teachers have difficulty fitting it all in. Identifying ways of bringing subjects together can certainly help (Davies *et al.* 2000). To summarise, both subjects, if taught well, involve children:

- engaging in processes systematically
- developing and applying common knowledge bases
- being creative – thinking laterally, linking ideas and being innovative
- identifying and solving problems – breaking problems down, sequencing and planning the best way to tackle them
- generating, developing and communicating ideas
- investigating materials and phenomena
- identifying variables and factors
- establishing criteria for testing and carrying out fair tests
- predicting
- estimating and measuring
- using tools, equipment and materials safely
- evaluating outcomes and the processes involved in reaching them
- reporting to a variety of audiences.

We might expect that children developing one or more of these capabilities in either design and technology or science might exhibit it in the other. This is not to imply that transfer of learning across subjects is straightforward – it isn't – but drawing children's attention to these common elements of learning may enable them to reflect upon and hence develop their own performance. The issue of skill transferability is revisited in Chapter 3.3.

The first section of this book established our view that design and technology is an intensely creative area of the curriculum, providing constant opportunities for children to act creatively. Others have made a similar case for science (Frost 1997; Johnston 1996). This aspect of both subjects needs promoting more vigorously. An interactionist approach to science and design and technology alongside linking these areas with other subjects (as discussed in Chapter 2.3) contributes to fostering new attitudes among children and colleagues to children's learning.

Consequently, we consider the advantages of making links between science and design and technology to be considerable. It helps children appreciate the relevance of science to everyday life and provides purpose for investigations. Learning in design and technology benefits from this since more systematic approaches to research, testing prototypes and evaluating outcomes can encourage thorough use of scientific enquiry. Linking them also increases the likelihood of learning being transferred effectively from one area to another. However, we are not suggesting that science should always be linked with design and technology or that design and technology should be taught in a way that values its link with science over those with other disciplines such as art. These decisions are an essential part of long-term planning, and are best done collaboratively by teaching staff. A balanced curriculum is likely to include some units of work where the links are strong; others where they are much more limited, if not non-existent.

For teachers needing help in identifying potential links, the QCA Scheme of Work for Design and Technology (QCA/DfEE 1998) provides examples of how links with the science curriculum can be made within each unit.

The following case study illustrates an approach to a project on torches aimed at maximising children's learning in both subjects.

Case Study 4 – Torches (Year 4)

Setting the scene
This work was carried out with a Year 4 class taught by Shoriza Clark at Durand Primary School in South London. The case study is based on an evaluation of a unit of work from the Nuffield Primary Design and Technology Project (Barlex 2000) developed by Dan Davies (this can be found at http://www.nuffieldfoundation.org/filelibrary/pdf/torch.pdf).

The teaching sequence

In session 1 children's ideas about torches, the purposes and operation were elicited with questions such as: 'What do torches do and why are they used?' 'Who uses torches?' 'Why are there so many different designs?' 'Do the designs tell us about who will use them?' The children then looked at a range of torches and took them apart (IEA), considering further questions: 'What material is each part made from?' 'What are the different parts?' 'How many batteries does the torch need?' They then drew a picture of the inside of the torch using labels to show how it worked and the electric circuit.

During session 2 the children tried to make the torch bulb light without using the casing. They drew the resulting circuit and found out what happens with more bulbs in their circuits (Sc 1). In session 3 attention turned to investigating and making switches (FPT).

The next three sessions were devoted to a DMA. A whole-class discussion led to sentence completion: My torch is for … It will be used by … It will be used at … with children producing a large drawing showing what their torch was to be like. Children chose the battery and switch and wired up their own circuit before building it into their torch. They considered how to make it work well, for example, by improving the shape of the reflector. They then focused on the overall appearance and making it look right.

In session 7 children evaluated their outcomes using the criteria that they set out at the beginning and made necessary improvements in the light of their evaluations.

Shoriza successfully implemented the series of lessons and the children produced a range of working outcomes. Many of the outcomes, such as a 'hat torch', were innovative and well-made products from which the children gained a great deal of satisfaction. Shoriza evaluated the work positively describing the children's sense of achievement as 'wonderful'. She considered the tasks appropriate for the age group and highly relevant to the electricity work that was planned for that term from the school SoW for Science. She identified specific learning outcomes for most pupils, highlighting their developing understanding of the need for good electrical connections, their skills in using tools safely and their perseverance. The need to apply their learning about simple circuits immediately in the context of making the torch was an ideal way of linking their science and design and technology. The children had some difficulties, for example, making sure that their circuits stayed connected – they used foil in several instances to overcome this problem. They also found that they needed to use commercial battery holders which did not always fit into the aesthetic case that they planned to use (although Shoriza realised later that the use of film canisters to hold 1.5v batteries would have solved this problem). She managed most sessions by dividing the class into two or three groups and providing self-managed activities for two groups so that she could concentrate on the third. She had found the teacher materials provided by the Nuffield unit extremely helpful, particularly appreciating the questions listed for her to ask the children. Shoriza had found that the use of the suggested story book (*Where Oh Where Is Kipper's Bear?* by Mick Inkpen) really inspired the children and motivated them. On reflection she felt more time was needed for the initial activity on investigating the torches, less time was needed on the circuits and switches (since it built on work the children had done in Key Stage 1) and more sessions were required for the making phase.

Discussion

This case study illustrates an interactionist approach; the starting point was a design and technology IEA (investigating torches and taking them apart), moving to a science-based input on electric circuits, following this with a FPT (making switches), then a DMA (making a torch) which required the knowledge and understanding gained to be applied. This approach fits well with our view of how children learn, the importance of meaningful contexts for activities, and the significance of the application of newly constructed understanding to reinforce the learning that has resulted from a scientific activity (Ollerenshaw and Ritchie 1997).

Ritchie (2001) provides another example, where the links between science and design and technology are strong but in this case the model is one where learning in science preceded the design and technology activity. Year 6 children had been learning about structures and strengthening materials in science and were challenged, a few weeks later, to design and make model air-raid shelters. There was encouraging evidence for the teacher, Richard Brice, of the children applying the knowledge and understanding they had gained and the opportunity with some children to revisit the ideas where misunderstanding became apparent. Additionally, Richard used the air-raid shelter activity to further develop the children's learning in Science 1 by getting them to develop fair tests to investigate the success of their outcomes. In this way, his approach also illustrated aspects of an interactionist approach.

An example of technology preceding science in a different way was used in a Bath school recently when engineering students from the university took along an energy-saving vehicle which they had recently designed and built to show pupils at St. Philip's Primary School. The visit led to discussions about how much fuel the innovative vehicle used compared with family cars and to questions of streamlining and use of materials. A critical note was struck by the pupils who commented on the vehicle's lack of comfort and space for shopping. There were opportunities resulting from the discussion for children to research the impact of cars on the environment and related issues of global warming. Such a visit could also be the stimulus for the children designing and making their own model fuel-conserving streamlined vehicles, which they could test through a systematic investigation – perhaps by dropping different shapes through a container of wallpaper paste to see which offers least drag. The use of a viscous liquid such as paste in this investigation serves to slow down the descent for each shape, making timing easier and more reliable.

In the torches case study, the teacher did not make it explicit when the children were doing science or design and technology. The teacher in the air-raid shelter project made this more explicit with his class. The children were aware when they were being scientists and when they were being designers. We do consider that it is appropriate at times for children to be made aware of the differences between the two subjects. Indeed, this becomes essential if, as we discuss below, children are taught to appreciate more about the nature of the subjects and their cultural significance.

Developing children's awareness and understanding of the impact of science and technology on their lives

Learning in design and technology has several purposes, such as the capability to use skills and knowledge and understanding in a range of contexts at school, at home and longer term in adult life including work. However, it is also about developing children's awareness of the implications of science and technology on society and individuals. This is stressed in the National Curriculum; for example, the statement entitled 'The Importance of Science' includes the following:

> Through science pupils understand how major scientific ideas contribute to technological change – impacting on industry, business and medicine and improving the quality of life. Pupils recognise the cultural significance of science and trace its worldwide development.

They learn to question and discuss science-based issues that may affect their own lives, the direction of society and the future of the world.

(DfEE/QCA 1999c: 76)

It is also addressed through the values statements about the environment in the National Curriculum (DfEE/QCA 1999c: 149). Raising children's awareness of human impact on the environment and the significance of science and technology within society are priorities for teachers of children of all ages.

Whether science and technology have had, and are having, a positive or negative impact on human society is a question that certainly has no simple answer. In any case, who is responsible: the scientists whose ideas or discoveries enabled the development or the technologists developing a technology with unforeseen effects? Perhaps the only consensus we could expect to find is that no one would suggest the impact of science and technology has been neutral or non-existent. Most people would agree that scientists and technologists should accept responsibility for their actions. So how do we deal with these questions with children? Below are some suggestions.

An interesting example of making the issues explicit for children was tried by Bristol local education authority (LEA) recently. Annually, a Children's Parliament is held in the Council House. Local primary school councils were invited to send along representatives to debate whether science and technology would, in their view, improve the world and our lives or not. The responses to the questions were surprisingly sophisticated and the children showed their developing understanding of the complexity of the questions being asked. They agreed that there was not a simple answer, although the result suggested that these children were genuinely concerned about the negative effects of science and technology and were cautioning adults to proceed with care with so-called advances.

School- or class-based debates about topical issues such as genetically modified (GM) crops, global warming (perhaps stimulated by local flooding/extreme weather), BSE or local issues, can be organised. Recently in one Year 4 class a student teacher, Roanne Legg, organised an 'inquiry' into the possible closure of the school access road. Advocates 'for' and 'against' were appointed and other children took the role of community groups – parents, tradespeople, residents etc. – who took the stand as witnesses. A good deal of preparatory work had been done to ensure the views expressed were informed. Children were very strong in their views and were surprisingly familiar with an adversarial approach to courtroom procedure. The debate gave rise to a DMA involving modelling automatic gates to restrict access to the school road.

Several websites have been set up to help children find out more about topical issues (e.g. http://whyfiles.org/). Setting up teams and organising the debate fairly formally, with a vote at the end, can increase the pupils' motivation. Explicit links with the design and technology curriculum might be related to food safety or the social, economic and environmental impact of a specific product (e.g. a mobile phone or disposable nappies). Young children at Key Stage 1 can be invited to talk about some of these issues if they are introduced in appropriate language, or through a story (such as Michael Foreman's *Dinosaurs and All That Rubbish*), and the discussion is handled sensitively. Section Three picks up these themes with case studies illustrating a range of projects intended to increase children's environmental awareness, their involvement in environmental projects and those related to health education as part of their citizenship education. Such projects clearly provide opportunities for teachers to raise issues explicitly about the direct impact human actions can have on our world and daily lives.

Another aspect of children's views of science and technology with implications for cultural understanding concerns their ideas about 'who' is involved. There is worrying evidence that children continue to think that scientists (and by association technologists) are white men with beards, wearing white coats. Jarvis and Rennie (2000: 7) claim these views are prevalent from about the age of eight, although this is not always the case (McMahon 1999). However, where such stereotypical views are held, they can be hard to change (especially as they can be evident more generally in society). Nevertheless, teachers' interventions can make a difference (Matthews and Davies 1999). Making the subjects more 'girl-friendly' (Browne 1991; Kelly 1987; Kirkup and Keller 1992) and providing examples and stories of scientific and technological achievements of women throughout history and in contemporary society can help to counter gender stereotypes. The stories of the chemist Dorothy Hodgkin and Marie Curie (Jarvis and Rennie 2000) are examples of this, as is the story of Mae Jemison, the first Afro-American woman astronaut. This raises another important strand to such stereotypical views: those concerning ethnocentricity. Chapter 2.4 deals with this issue more fully, but it is important at this stage of our discussion to raise the need for teachers to challenge such views and provide evidence to support this challenge. This means using examples of achievements from a range of historical and cultural contexts involving groups and individuals from a variety of ethnic groups. Jarvis and Rennie (2000) provide an excellent set of pictures of technologists including the able-bodied and people with disabilities from a range of ethnic groups, which can be used to stimulate discussion. Children growing up in Britain's multicultural society should not be given a narrow view of science and technology that implies the superiority of one group over another.

Children's evolving cultural awareness and understanding also relate to the way in which they and others perceive the relative importance and value of different areas of learning. Are children growing up in a society that privileges some domains of learning over others? This is discussed in Chapter 2.3 with regard to the relationship between design and technology and the arts. In our education system, it appears that English, mathematics and pure sciences are seen as having a higher status than design and technology. Certainly, in the not too distant past, the science department in a secondary school would have had higher status than the design and technology department. The confirmation of science as a core curriculum subject and design and technology as a foundation subject when the National Curriculum was introduced (DES/WO 1988) reinforced this.

The divide between 'thinkers' and 'doers' is deeply entrenched in our culture and goes back as far as Ancient Greece, if not earlier. It is still reflected in many contemporary views. The current debate about post-16 education and the difference between academic and vocational studies relates, in some ways, to this divide. Compare society's views on illiteracy and technological incompetence; no one feels embarrassed or ashamed of not being able to programme the video or understand why a car engine needs oil in the right reservoir. With science and technology playing an increasingly important part in our lives, isn't it time to redress the balance? This theme will be revisited in the next chapter.

Jarvis and Rennie's (2000) publication, *Helping Children Understand, Science and Technology*, sets out useful guidelines for teachers in order to help children recognise that:

- men and women scientists and technologists work in a wide variety of occupations and locations throughout the world

- scientific ideas have been used in the design and production of most manufactured items

- all manufactured items are technological products made by people

- new scientific ideas will influence how future products are developed

- scientists and technologists must and do consider the consequences of their discoveries and take some responsibility for them.

This is an important agenda for teachers. It should inform planning for design and technology if teaching is to go beyond the effective to become truly creative.

Summary

This chapter is based on the premise that children's cultural education should involve them learning about the nature of science and technology and their impact on everyday lives and society. We have explored the relationship between the subjects and advocated an interactionist approach wherever appropriate to foster close links that benefit learning in both areas.

There are many dimensions to the cultural impact of science and technology that we have sought to highlight. These cover issues related to: gender; ethnocentricity and Eurocentricity; the impact of development on the environment, individuals and groups of people; and the relative value and status of different endeavours in society. These are challenging areas in many ways for both teachers and children. It is our view that primary education, if it is to provide a broad and balanced cultural education for children, is a phase in which such issues should be raised and explored through the relevant contexts that design and technology has to offer.

The relationship between design and technology and the arts

Purpose of this chapter

Through reading this chapter you will gain:

- a critical appreciation of the cultural significance of the arts
- an understanding of the relationship between design and technology and the arts in school
- an insight into ways in which teachers have provided opportunities for pupils to experience these links and through those experiences develop their cultural knowledge and understanding.

Introduction

The term 'creative arts' is often used to describe subjects such as drama, music and art and design. It implies that some subjects are more creative than others and promotes a misconception about the nature of creativity. We have already argued that design and technology should be regarded as a creative subject (Chapter 1.2). In this chapter we intend to develop this discussion further. We shall look at the relationship between design and technology and the arts and show how an interactionist approach discussed in the previous chapter can benefit children's learning and help break down stereotypical views about whether particular areas of learning are creative or not.

A socially constructed divide between the arts and technology has been around for a long time. Snow (1959) discussed it in terms of 'two cultures', asserting that academic life is strictly divided between 'artists' and 'scientists'. Arts often seem to have a higher cultural standing in society – someone who engages in or appreciates technological development is unlikely to be considered cultured in the same way as someone who makes music or appreciates opera. There is no 'technologists' corner' in Westminster Abbey. Curiously, the *Shorter Oxford Dictionary* defines technology as 'the scientific study of the practical and industrial arts'. This suggests that the divide may not be as stark as often imagined. It is our contention that schools should contribute to changing attitudes towards design and technology, through recognising its creative dimension and its importance in everyday life. This can be done best by fostering the links between design and technology and arts subjects in schools, rather than trying to set one above another in importance.

Chapter 2.1 introduced a very broad definition of culture and located the development of children's cultural awareness, knowledge and understanding within a framework of 'the shared values and patterns of behaviour that characterises different social groups and communities' (NACCCE 1999: 42). It is a much more elitist view of culture that is implied when people are described as cultured. This usually refers to individuals' awareness of, or involvement with, 'high' culture such as classical music, conventional theatre and opera. We will explore the contribution that design and technology can make to extending children's experience into such areas and broadening their cultural appreciation and understanding. This will include further discussion of the concept of visual literacy introduced in Section One. However, for many children (and adults) the concept of popular culture has more resonance with their everyday lives and interests. The ways in which design and technology can link with children's everyday cultural experiences (such as the use of new technologies in popular music or the creation of animations) is another area that has more potential than is often explored in schools.

Linking design and technology with drama

Most schools provide opportunities for children to become involved in drama and this often includes school productions. While such productions are by no means sufficient drama education, they are often powerful experiences for children that are remembered long after learning associated with more traditional lessons is forgotten. Dramatic productions might be spontaneous and unrehearsed or carefully staged, involving considerable preparation. Both extremes provide opportunities for design and technology while contributing to children's cultural development. The following case study illustrates an ambitious attempt by two teachers to stage a Shakespearean production which they planned to provide rich experiences for developing children's learning in design and technology.

Case Study 5 – Staging *A Midsummer Night's Dream* (Year 6)

At Christchurch Primary School in Bradford-on-Avon, Year 6 are taught by Sarah Jackson, Bev Ball and Judith Cock. The following work was organised in a six-week period after the SATs in the summer term. The outcome was an impressive performance of *A Midsummer Night's Dream.*

The choice of play was the teachers', but the children soon threw themselves into the project and took ownership of many aspects of the production. It began with a mini-enterprise activity involving the children in making cakes (at home and school) to sell in order to raise money for the scripts that they needed to buy.

However, the main design and technology aspects of the work involved the costumes and props. To stimulate the children's ideas about costumes and to provide some background research opportunities, both classes watched a cartoon version of the play and a live action production on video. They also used reference books to research the background to the play and the period in which it was set. The teachers stressed the need for simple costumes that were appropriate for the characters. As a design exercise, the teachers put the names of all the characters on the board and invited the children to choose one on which to focus. They were then asked to draw some initial ideas for 'their' characters. A large sheet of paper was provided for each character (or group, such as 'Workers'). Children who produced a design proposal or several that they liked then stuck them on the appropriate sheet. Some of these were annotated to indicate materials to be used – for example costumes for the 'Royals' had, in the words of one child, 'to be posh fabrics'. Where children were working on the same character they were encouraged to collaborate. This session produced a wide range of creative ideas and certainly helped the children focus on simple designs that could be made relatively easily – a lot of costumes had to be made as there were over 35 fairies alone.

The next stage of the project was organised as weekly workshops. Four of these were arranged in different rooms or spaces. One group tackled costumes for the Royals, another concentrated on Fairies, a third on Workers and the final group on 'banners'. Children from both classes were allocated to the various groups. The workshops lasted for whole afternoons during which the children developed and produced the costumes. They chose whom to make the costume for (parts in the play having by then been assigned to individuals) and began by taking the necessary measurements. They then made the costumes with appropriate skills being taught by the adults as necessary. The children had limited experience of work with textiles so making the costumes involved them developing and using a range of skills including cutting fabric accurately, pinning, sewing, hemming, adding adornments, using fabric paints, using Velcro and other fastenings, gluing etc. Some children were taught to use the sewing machine that was available in one workshop area. After several sessions' work, with considerable changes in design on the way, the costumes were tried on the actors. At this stage, evaluation comments from the wearer were used to refine and, in one or two cases, dramatically change the costumes. One girl insisted on having trousers made rather than wearing tights. Some very frank feedback was offered to the designers – particularly when it came to colour coordination for the Royals. In some cases the actors decided to make changes once they had assumed ownership of the costume. For example, one child decided to add additional ties all the way down the side of his costume since the single ties originally planned proved inadequate to keep the costume in place as he moved around quickly.

Once costumes were completed, a range of cardboard animal masks was made using a wide variety of materials including feathers, fur fabric, leather, foil, felt, pipe-cleaners and various threads. Pictures from books provided the main stimulus for these masks, which were made to fit individual children offering more opportunities to apply measuring skills. Props were made using techniques such as papier mâché and three-dimensional cardboard modelling. The workers made 'tools' to carry. Armour for one of the Royals was designed with particular help from a child who turned out to have a fascination with and considerable knowledge about armour. An automated donkey's head was made (with help from an adult) which had ears that moved backwards and forwards remotely from off-stage using recycled parts of a broken remote controlled car. The scenery was also substantially influenced by the children's ideas. One child had the idea of using camouflage material that he had at home to create the forest – the use of small Christmas tree lights added a magical touch.

When asked what they thought of the experience of producing their own costumes and props there was a general consensus that it was fun and far better than being given ready-made outfits. The children's enthusiasm and perseverance was impressive. They liked being given responsibility for making decisions about what they would create and were generally very pleased with the results. Crucially, they reflected that making the costumes had made them think about the characters in the play more than they might have done. Several referred to the stark contrast between the richness of the Royals' outfits (in one case special embroidered fabric was purchased to achieve the desired result) and the simple clothes of the workers (which were also rough to the touch and uncomfortable to wear).

Discussion

Such an experience for these children is likely to have left them with a significant impression about their capacity to be successful and creative. Because of the emphasis placed on design and technology during the production, their views about their creativity will have been associated with learning in that subject. Additionally, the effort put into thinking about costumes and props and having to make them will have increased their understanding of the play's themes and the period in which it was set. The outcome was one shared with parents and other members of the school community. It became a celebration at a significant time in their school career. Moving from primary to secondary education is a rite of passage for all children. These children took with them into their secondary education a very positive experience in which design and technology had played an important part.

Making costumes and props for school productions is often a job taken on by parents or other adults working in school. Such an approach wastes an excellent opportunity for children to be involved in real design and technology, engaging with a need that they can easily recognise and offering a genuine purpose for their designing and making. Ritchie (2001) provides another example of drama being linked to design and technology in his examples of children taking responsibility for staging a Roman feast and Greek games (involving work on costumes, props, food and rituals). He also discusses in detail a case study that involved Reception class children producing puppets to use in a class assembly. Case Study 10 (Chapter 3.2) provides another example of children designing and making puppets for use in retelling traditional tales. The QCA Scheme of Work (QCA/DfEE 1998) includes a unit (2D) – 'Joseph's coat' – the emphasis of which is on children producing prototype garments. This could be adapted, with perhaps Year 2 pupils working in collaboration with older children, to involve the making of a coat to be used in a production. Shadow puppets provide an opportunity for the use of mechanisms to control movement through which children can tell their own stories or retell those of others, including traditional tales from a range of cultures. Children can be particularly good at scripting their own soap operas, based, perhaps, on characters found in a school! Further examples are included in Chapter 3.2.

Linking design and technology with art

Design and technology could be seen as closely related to art and design in the National Curriculum (as the inclusion of design in the title of both would suggest). There are also close parallels to the way in which artists and designers work. In both domains there is likely to be a need or want identified (perhaps by a client or by the maker him/herself), incubation and generating ideas phases involving the modelling or sketching of ideas. Both involve making and constant critical evaluation, drawing on a knowledge of materials. These similarities of process should not blind us to the distinct *purposes* underlying the two disciplines however, as the following example demonstrates.

Baxendall (1985), writing about two very recognisable, yet seemingly very different products of design and technology (the Forth Bridge) and art (Picasso's *Portrait of Kahnweiler* – a cubist portrait of a male friend), draws fascinating parallels between these two outcomes of human creativity. He claims that:

> Both are purposeful objects and are not necessarily different. The differences seem more of degree and of balance, particularly the balance of our interests and of our critical priorities.
>
> (Baxendall 1985: 40)

Baxendall argues that in coming to understand the two objects, and ultimately the mind of the artist or designer, a common process is evident. Whether or not the decision maker sees him/herself as an artist or designer, both will make decisions based on constraints. One of the constraints of bridge-building is the brief, depending on specifics such as the location of towns, the nature of the traffic that will use the bridge and the local weather conditions that a structure will need to withstand. In Picasso's era, the brief of an artist was personally constructed within a cultural framework. In other words, no client was involved and no negotiation with others was needed. Yet Picasso's contact with his society, his circle of friends and critics and the long tradition of painting as a human endeavour would greatly influence his work. Of course, many artists do not have the luxury of constructing an entirely personal brief. More often concerns such as critical acclaim, commercial appeal – even the demands of a client – will feature in the work of many artists, craftworkers and designers.

Another of Baxendall's criteria by which to distinguish the purpose of 'designerly' or artistic endeavour is what he refers to as *causes of form*. For Picasso, causes of form would be matters such as the pigments and colours available (media) and perhaps a new way of representing objects introduced by Cezanne. He was also influenced by knowledge about African sculpture from a recent exhibition, the critical reception of his earlier work *Demoiselles d'Avignon*, and reaction against the preoccupations of the Impressionists. For the bridge designer, causes of form would include the materials available at the time, the cost of the materials, the recent (at the time) occurrences of bridge failures and the prevalent aesthetic of massive and impressive structures. These constraints are as influential today as they were in the Victorian era – one only has to look to the Millennium footbridge across the Thames to the Tate Modern for a case study.

From this examination of the work of artist and designer, one can draw strong parallels between the ways in which creative people work. We are not saying that the two subjects are the same, yet when they are considered as creative processes influenced by culture, in primary classrooms there are a number of fundamental features they have in common. Indeed if one looks at the QCA/DfEE Schemes of Work (1998, 2000b) for the two subjects, there are several common terms used – exploring and developing ideas, investigating, designing, modelling, considering the user, evaluating. It is not acceptable to claim that the terms have different meanings in the two domains – that surely is too confusing for learners and teachers alike. The two subjects should be taught in such a way that the approaches are complementary and make a coherent contribution to creative and cultural development.

The making of Christmas cards is a common activity in which learning in these two areas might be addressed while developing children's visual literacy (see Chapter 2.1). Figure 2.3.1 shows how a collection of cards can be investigated. The questions direct attention to the aesthetic aspects of the card, which are, of course, culturally determined. It then requires the children to write a design brief based on their investigation. In this way the making of the card can also fulfil aspects of the design and technology programme of study associated with the development of designing skills.

Depending on the techniques used to produce the cards, aspects of the making section of the curriculum might also be addressed.

---

1. Use the whole collection of cards to answer the following:

Which categories or genres of Yuletide imagery can you identify? E.g. traditional (Renaissance) Christian, humorous, winter scene etc.

Which art techniques are evident? E.g. collage, oil painting, photography, water colour

Which styles can you see? E.g. realistic, stylised, abstract

Which colours are prevalent? E.g. red hues, tints (light/mixed with white), saturated, complementary

Which subjects are common?

Which formats are used? E.g. landscape, with border, framed, shaped

2. Using the religious cards and books only

Which subjects are common? E.g. Jesus, Joseph, candles, stars

Which colours are prevalent?

How are the colours used? E.g. gold to highlight, blue for Mary

How are the pictures composed to draw the eye to the picture or part of the picture? E.g. use of line, use of gesture, use of light/tone, use of colour

3. Write some specifications for the brief: 'A Christmas picture in a traditional Christian style'.

Figure 2.3.1 Investigating Christmas cards – imagery and composition

The following case study extends this approach, employing an interactionist approach to the subjects while contributing to children's cultural understanding.

Case Study 6 – Using Hogarth's painting *The Graham Children* (whole school)

Horton Primary School is a small rural school in South Gloucestershire where the combined class of 7–11-year-old pupils is taught by Claire Garven and Valerie Downes, and the infants are taught by Joanne Dent. This case study features the approach of the Key Stage 2 teachers and their children, although the younger children worked in a similar way on modified tasks. The head teacher, Hilary Pride, is very keen to provide opportunities for the children to see and appreciate artworks. Last year art was a priority for development, so she arranged for the whole staff to attend an in-service education and training (INSET) day at the National Gallery in London, which focused on encouraging schools to use works on art with children. This was part of a national initiative that the National Gallery runs each year. Schools that attend such days are provided with a high quality copy of one of the paintings in the collection. Last year all schools were given a copy of Hogarth's *The Graham Children*. Rather than just leave it on the wall for the children to look at, the teachers planned more active ways of engaging the children with the painting through a variety of activities in several curriculum areas, including design and technology. Children were organised in groups and asked to create model rooms (in large cardboard boxes) based on the period in which *The Graham Children* was painted, and to model the children featured. This activity involved the children in developing a number of skills related to work with resistant materials and textiles. It required them to focus on the details and clues they could see in the picture and use other sources to research the period. Their outcomes were original and creative products in their own right. To bring the work into the modern era and link with the children's understanding of popular culture, the teachers then asked the groups to think about what a contemporary setting for such a picture might involve. The original is very formally posed but their ideas for new compositions included, in several cases, technological props such as a portable CD player and games consoles. They wanted the children portrayed to be seen as active rather than passive as in the original. One group decided to set their 'picture' on the beach, with appropriate dress and props. The teachers developed the activity in two ways. Initially the groups had to set up their scenes using real or modelled artefacts with children dressed in appropriate clothes. They then had their photographs taken by another child using the school's digital camera, which led to discussions about the present-day equivalent of the painted portrait (at least in the experience of most people). The children modified and printed the portraits for display. They then created their own works of art (collaboratively in their original groups) using the photographs as the stimulus. The results were framed (again by the children using their own ideas for contemporary frames). The resulting work produced impressive displays around the school. A a follow-up to the INSET day, schools had been invited to send in a report of work carried out based on the painting. These were to be followed up by visits from National Gallery staff which were intended to identify children's work that could be displayed in the National Gallery; any school whose work was selected would get an expenses-paid visit for children, teachers and parents to see the display. Horton's report led to a visit by National Gallery staff and some very positive feedback.

Discussion

Unfortunately the school was not lucky enough to win the visit to London. Despite this, there is no doubt in the teachers' minds that the project was a success and that the children gained a well-founded appreciation of Hogarth's work. The children had an opportunity to develop an aspect of their visual literacy during the project in that they had been introduced to a way in which a picture can be investigated and analysed. To create the three-dimensional models required very careful observation of the painting. The children also had opportunities to consider the role and intention of the artist in setting the scene, and the social status of the family. The cultural setting of portraiture had been explored. The children had been given some of the keys with which to unlock the meanings of this particular cultural form of representation.

Linking design and technology with music

No discussion of design and technology's links with the arts would be complete without considering music. An obvious activity here is the designing and making of musical instruments (see Chapter 2.4). A less obvious example is that of children writing and producing their own opera. The following case study has some features similar to the previous two, but introduces the element of creating and performing music, as well as taking considerable managerial responsibility for a piece of high culture.

Case Study 7 – The *Dark Sea Mystery* opera

This case study describes a project based in St. Luke's CE Primary School, South London involving Dan Davies and head teacher Helen Quintrell. They had both attended a course during an Easter holiday at the Royal Opera House on 'Creating Original Opera' and returned to school inspired to give it a try. Dan was keen to ensure the work had a strong design and technology dimension and therefore involved a professional stage designer, Francis O'Connor, in the project. The project, implemented with Dan's class of Year 5 children, was planned to provide learning opportunities in English, maths, science, design and technology, art and design and music. Work with the children began in October and the production was staged the following February. Parents were sent letters outlining what was intended and emphasising the curriculum work that would be covered. The first stage was to engage the children in the writing process: establishing a theme, thesis, characters and conflicts for the piece. There was a strong democratic approach to these early decisions involving, at times, secret ballots. This ensured ownership of the project by the children. In early November children applied and were interviewed for jobs within a 'production company' using the school's equal opportunities interviewing procedures. A class visit to the Theatre Museum, Covent Garden, was arranged where the children learnt more about the roles of director, producer, stage manager etc. that they had taken on. On the same day, the children also visited the Royal Opera House to see how set designs evolve from model room to construction workshop ready for a final fit-up on stage. The Best Opera Company was formed, involving a clear management structure and groups in the following departments: creative; design/technical; performance and public relations. The child taking the role of production manager held regular meetings with the various teams. He managed the budget using a spreadsheet. Grants were obtained, including £1000 from the South London Education Business Partnership for portable stage lighting. It was also the production manager's role to produce a rehearsal schedule and he recorded progress using the school's video camera. He wrote an introductory speech which he delivered at the performance. The stage manager had a key job during auditions – making decisions about who should get which part. She led some of the rehearsals and ran warm-up sessions for the cast. Another part of her job involved responsibility for the collection or construction of props.

The whole-class discussions had led to a pollution theme for the opera, something that was very important to the children. A plot was devised to involve five main characters with specific attributes: for example one generous, another bad-tempered. The writers' group developed this theme into a brief three-act scenario. Some of the characters were humans on an oil rig, others were sea creatures affected by an oil spillage. The writing, using word processors, included individual and collaborative work. Once the ideas had been redrafted, the children split into pairs to work on a libretto for the opera, comprising dialogue and lyrics. This took a month and went through seven drafts. Music was produced using an electronic keyboard and pitched percussion instruments, improvising sound patterns that conveyed various moods and settings (such as an underwater environment with an element of threat). A musical motif was written for each character for entrances and exits. ICT played a part in that some of the composition used 'Compose' software. When the score was complete, the composers drafted in extra children (and staff) to form the orchestra. The piece was rehearsed conscientiously until it was ready for live performance.

Set design and construction

The set design team initially discussed the theme, visual identity (how the total production would look) and concept of the opera with the director (Dan), production manager and writers. At the Opera House, Francis O'Connor showed them how professional designers translate their concepts into detailed 1:25 scale three-dimensional models. Back at school the children's research involved collecting pictures, photos and information about the marine world and oil rigs from magazines and books, together with their notes from the exhibition they had seen at the Theatre Museum, before producing a range of sketches, paintings and collages. They discussed with Francis how these early ideas could relate to the scenario developed by the writers. He helped them clarify their ideas and establish a consistent style which would run through the design of the whole set.

In accordance with the professional practice they had observed, the children then measured and constructed a scale model of the performance space. This provided a model box within which they could build different versions of their set to investigate which of the juxtapositions of various scenery elements would be likely to be most effective. They decided that a 'thrust stage' with seating on three sides would improve sight lines for an audience within the low-ceilinged dining hall. The final version of the model box was presented to Francis and the rest of the company during a production meeting. This helped to inform the writers developing the script, as the design incorporated in the same space scenes that took place both under and on the surface of the sea.

The design team now met with the carpenters to draw up a list of resources needed to build the set. They visited local timber yards, DIY merchants, car spares and carpet shops, and made requests for materials in the school newsletter. The set was built in sections over the months of January and February, one group being responsible for structures (e.g. a giant oil rig leg which formed the crux of the design), another for plastic sheeting and drapes (sprayed with green and blue car paint to simulate an undersea environment), and a third team for the backdrop, a collage of green refuse sacks, torn in strips to give the crinkled edges of seaweed. Francis visited twice: early in the process to give advice on materials and fixing techniques, and towards the end to supervise the final fit-up of the set in the hall.

Costume design
This team worked from the writers' descriptions of the characters, making a number of sketches which they felt emphasised the attributes specified. In discussion with the director and writers they gained a firmer idea of who the characters were, and went on to use visual material on sea creatures from magazines and books, together with costume designs from the Covent Garden exhibition to produce large colour images of each character in costume. In discussion with Francis they decided on the fabrics and other materials needed to realise their designs (e.g. yellow refuse sacks for the fish) and annotated their drawings to inform the making process. Other members of the company were asked to bring in particular pieces of old clothing that could be adapted using fabrics, plastics and silver marker pens. Other children were drafted in to help in the production of costumes over a period of several weeks. The final creations were labelled and hung on a wardrobe rail ready for the production. The costume design team had to check and maintain the costumes after each performance (Fig. 2.3.2).

The team of 'electricians', working with a drama student, first researched the safety aspects of electricity (building simple switched

Figure 2.3.2 Children model costumes for the *Dark Sea Mystery* opera

circuits and finding out about watts, amps and volts from books) before writing their own company safety policy. They also explored different ways of suggesting location, time and mood using stage lighting effects. They next bought electrical components and constructed a set of footlights, which was checked by a professional electrician before connection to their dimmer board. They also borrowed spotlights and floodlights from a local theatre centre. Following this they watched a rehearsal and annotated their copy of the script, deciding on the effects they wanted and writing in lighting cues. They discussed with the set designers how the lighting could most effectively integrate with the scenery (e.g. by positioning some lights behind translucent screens to give a diffused underwater effect) and controlled the dimmer board during the performances.

All of the children involved took responsibility for their contribution – from make-up designers to public relations – all were committed, all shared in the success (and the extensive local publicity that resulted), all enjoyed the experience and all gained an increased understanding of opera and an appreciation of the complexity and creativity involved in its production. Pauline Tambling, the Education Officer from the Royal Opera House, wrote the following to the children after seeing the performance: 'It was a wonderful performance and I thought you had covered all aspects of the production remarkably well. I have seen nearly a hundred performances by groups of pupils in schools and I thought yours was the best I have ever seen'. A review in the *Times Educational Supplement (TES)* called it 'an imaginatively staged piece with some attractive music ... this was a project which fostered creativity, self-confidence and a sense of responsibility' (*TES* April 1994).These children will never forget the experience.

Discussion

This was clearly a very ambitious project that required considerable effort and commitment from the teacher and head teacher involved, but there were many benefits for them and the school generally. These included developing excellent links with the local and wider community and raising the school's profile. Although it is unrealistic to expect many schools to implement projects on this scale, there are ways in which various aspects of it could be organised on a smaller scale. A particular strength was the involvement of a design-related professional to stimulate and support the children (see Chapter 1.4).

Linking design and technology with traditional and contemporary literature

Teachers have often used children's literature as a stimulus or context for design and technology. The potential for such activities to contribute to children's cultural understanding is less often promoted. Classic texts, such as Dickens' *Oliver Twist*, can be brought alive with activities such as designing and making typical suppers that might have been served in the workhouse. This can be used to explore some of the issues about class differences and poverty in Victorian England. Another example is the story of *Robinson Crusoe*, part of our cultural heritage that can be used as the theme of a topic in which children can think about dealing with the problems of life on a desert island, perhaps by designing and making essential artefacts or reflecting on the technological features of their own life they would miss most on the island.

Examples of using contemporary children's fiction as starting points for design and technology are discussed elsewhere (Lewisham LEA 1999; Ritchie 2001). *Charlie and the Chocolate Factory* by Roald Dahl is a well-established children's favourite with scope for design and technology links such as making chocolate machines or modelling the factory. Younger children can be challenged to help Mr Grinling (*The Lighthouse Keeper's Catastrophe* by Ronda and David Armitage) solve problems posed in a fictional context. Making books of a particular genre or for a specified audience (e.g. pop-up books, 'feely' books for younger readers) are well-established design and technology activities. Chapter 2.4 refers to other examples of children's fiction with a stronger multicultural dimension.

Design and technology work involving popular culture and folk traditions

The significance of popular culture and local traditions to children was noted at the beginning of this chapter. Case Study 6 (Hogarth's *The Graham Children*) illustrated a creative way in which one school linked classical art and popular culture successfully. This section will consider other ways in which design and technology activities might contribute to children's understanding and appreciation of popular culture. In Case Study 7 the children found writing a script for the opera relatively easy because of their familiarity with soap operas on television. We sometimes underestimate the amount children learn and gain from involvement in popular culture. Teachers often exploit children's familiarity with different genres of popular music, such as rap, in literacy and music lessons. What is possible in terms of design and technology? Packaging is an area with potential – children can use ICT to produce CD and cassette labels, perhaps including scanned photographs, clip art or photos taken with a digital camera. These can be adapted to package personalised versions of their favourite music, or labels for their own original creations. An example from a Bristol school involved a class producing a tape of songs heard at the local football ground (which required some censoring!) packaged in a cassette box with a label including the team's logo (with permission) and picture. A similar outcome could be a collection of playground games, chants or Christmas carols. Once a product has been prototyped or produced the next stage might be to produce an advertisement for it. In one school a class of Year 5 children was given such a task. Groups of children produced scripts, slogans, backgrounds and costumes (a considerable challenge in the case of the parrot food commercial along the lines of the *Whiskas* advert – eight out of ten parrots ...). The resulting short videos showed very clearly how aware the children had become of the strategies used by advertisers to promote their products.

To capitalise on children's familiarity with local radio and television, they can produce their own school radio or TV programme with an audio-tape recorder or video camera if the school has one. An ambitious approach to this could involve the construction of a TV studio set and the allocation of different roles as described in the opera project. Radio and TV formats can be used as a means for children to report on work from other curriculum areas. For example, children could produce a taped radio programme or TV news-slot reporting the findings of a scientific investigation that they have completed. For schools that have international links, the exchange of audio or video tapes or computer files is an excellent way of communicating and sharing 'cultures' – favourite songs, poems or TV programmes. Another task could involve children in both countries producing a tape of a typical day, including snippets from significant parts of the day, e.g. breakfast, starting school, morning break, lunchtime, getting home, an evening activity, bedtime. Such activities engage children with information technology in its broadest sense.

The success of animated films such as *Wallace and Gromit* (Aardman Animations) offers another stimulus for children to produce their own unique contribution to contemporary culture. Many school computers are now fast enough, with sufficient memory to allow children to use appropriate software to create their own animated films. For example, software is available for children to produce their own episodes of *The Simpsons* – the program offers visual and audio units which children can link together based on their own storyboard ideas. Such activities should be used to increase their understanding of the technologies involved, but equally importantly, as an opportunity to increase their critical faculties: what do they like about the media and its use and why? What do they dislike or disapprove of and why?

On the theme of new technologies, websites are increasingly making a contribution to contemporary culture – the NESTA web pages (www.nesta.org.uk) provide a good example of how websites are fast becoming 'works of art'. Children are increasingly being given opportunities in some schools to create or contribute to school websites.

Local and national traditions provide another cultural context for designing and making activities. In many schools, May Day still involves dancing around the pole (especially in rural schools). Costumes and props for such traditions can be the focus of design and technology. More will be said about religious festivals and carnivals in the next chapter.

Summary

This chapter has discussed the ways in which design and technology can foster children's understanding of cultural experiences that involve the arts. We have explored examples of design and technology activities that illustrate links with drama, visual art, music and literature. The case studies have focused on traditional and high culture such as classical theatre and opera. However, we have also highlighted the potential for using design and technology within the context of popular and contemporary culture. This has emphasised the opportunities that exist for new technologies to be used in these areas.

Learning within and about different cultures and traditions

Purpose of this chapter

Through reading this chapter you will gain:

- an awareness of the importance of multicultural dimensions to design and technology in the context of children's cultural understanding
- an understanding of the differences between multicultural and anti-racist approaches to design and technology
- an insight into the ways in which teachers can include multicultural and anti-racist dimensions within their design and technology teaching.

Introduction

This chapter will discuss different contexts in which design and technology activities can be set to foster children's awareness and understanding of other cultures, times and places. One aim of this is for children to learn to value and respect diversity, another is to offer them new perspectives through which to see their own lives and to inform their designing and making. We consider that one benefit of design and technology education is in the contribution it can make to cultural education (Chapter 2.1). We are also seeking to reinforce the inextricable links between creative and cultural education since creative processes 'draw directly from the cultural contexts in which they take place' (NACCCE 1999: 52). We will address differences between multicultural and anti-racist approaches to design and technology. Anti-racist approaches build on multicultural education but include strategies to confront explicitly potentially racist attitudes and behaviours.

Design and technology in its cultural and historical context

In Chapter 2.1, we provided a broad definition of culture and cultural education, recognising the range of cultures experienced by children in Britain. The richness and diversity of that multi-ethnic and multicultural society is something to be celebrated and valued. It is, however, also one that sadly involves explicit and implicit racism. The nature of our society and the cultures associated with it are, in part, the result of history and the mobility of human beings over many generations. If design and technology is to support children's cultural awareness and understanding, it is essential that teachers provide learning experiences that reflect cultural diversity and confront racism. This is important regardless of the particular composition of any individual class or school – cultural diversity provides opportunities for all in a truly inclusive society. However, for schools that include pupils from a range of ethnic backgrounds the benefits can be even greater, through ensuring that design and technology is relevant to all children and that all have equal access to the opportunities it provides. The Swann Report (DES/WO 1985: 3) stated that 'membership of a particular ethnic group is one of the most important aspects of an individual's identity – in how he or she perceives him or herself and in how he or she is perceived by others'. The valuing of children's home cultures in school can make a significant contribution to how valued the child feels. This affects their self-esteem, which clearly impacts on children's achievements.

The National Curriculum Council (1990a), in its guidance accompanying the original National Curriculum Orders, stressed that 'introducing multicultural perspectives into the curriculum is a way of enriching the education of all our pupils. It gives pupils the opportunities to view the world from different standpoints, helping them to question prejudice and developing open-mindedness' (1990a: 2). Such aspirations are still important. It is disappointing, in some ways, that more recent versions of the National Curriculum for design and technology have left multicultural aspects implicit rather than making them explicit. They were much more evident in the first version in which, for example, attainment target 1 – Identifying Needs and Opportunities – required pupils to explain how 'different cultures have influenced design and technology both in the needs met and opportunities identified'. Likewise, attainment target 4 – Evaluating – referred to pupils knowing that 'in the past and in other cultures people have used design and technology to solve familiar problems in different ways' (DES/WO 1990).

The historical influences on our technological society are clearly significant and provide another priority for teachers to address in developing children's cultural understanding. In the words of Siraj-Blatchford (1996: 9), 'The technologies that we encounter in our lives today are the product of value judgements in the past ... an essential element of an education in design and technology involves providing some understanding of the range of value options that have been considered, and an account of the reasons for the choices that have been made between them'. If teachers have a Eurocentric, industrial view of technology, this is likely to be the view passed on to children. Historically, many cultures around the world have developed technologies long before Europeans. For example, the Chinese used sophisticated navigation techniques based on the compass; the Egyptians used mechanisms to make work easier in order to construct pyramids; in India various innovative systems for cooling buildings, food and drinks were developed.

There were significant historical differences within Europe as well. Siraj-Blatchford highlights an interesting contrast between Pompeii (destroyed in AD 79) where excavations indicate that the Romans had sophisticated technology related to plumbing and heating, and Britain in 1951 where over a third of households lacked any form of fixed bath fitting (1996: 5). He reminds us that 'cultural chauvinism runs deep', and suggests that it is 'time we put technology in its place'. In other words, it is a responsibility of teachers to ensure that the design and technology education they offer children takes account of the history of technology, its global dimension and its impact on societies. This should help children 'grasp the many ways in which different cultures have long intersected and shaped each other' (NACCCE 1999: 51).

Another reason for adopting such an approach to design and technology is that, as discussed in Chapter 2.2, technology often creates winners and losers. This, in part, results from European imperialism in the past and highlights the need for a global perspective. The losers are often from under-represented groups, including women, black people and those with disabilities. Technology, developed and exploited in countries in the north (those sometimes inappropriately labelled as 'Developed') can also have adverse effects on cultures in other parts of the world, especially the east and south (those inappropriately labelled as 'Third World' or 'Underdeveloped'). Design and technology education provides the opportunity to help children develop a global perspective (see Chapters 3.1 and 3.4).

Adopting a multicultural approach

Multicultural education involves approaches to curriculum planning and implementation that recognise and address the multicultural society in which we live and the increasingly global dimension to people's lives. It requires teachers to set contexts and provide resources and information that do this. Through design and technology, five key ideas related to multicultural education (suggested by Loeb *et al.* 1993) can be addressed.

First, we want children *to learn to value, respect and celebrate diversity.* A danger in education is that we present other cultures in a way that offers a tokenistic or exotic view of another culture. This can be a result of presenting artefacts or customs in a decontextualised way, e.g. looking at an African mask, or making a First American 'god's-eye' without presenting to the children at some stage the story of precisely where the item came from, who made it and why. It is only in presenting an account of the artefact, its acquisition and its meaning to the individual who might have owned it or used it, that its value can be understood. The information need not be made available immediately; it may be possible for the children themselves to go some way to finding out information by looking at the artefact for clues. Young children will need considerable help to do this but children in Key Stage 2 will have begun to develop more knowledge on which to draw.

Secondly, for children to *appreciate that objects can be seen in response to common problems posed by the needs of society or individuals* will lead them to a fruitful comparison of solutions. One might take as a starting point a common problem such as the carrying and storage of food. Children will have experience of this particular issue and be able to contribute ideas and perhaps artefacts to a collection. The teacher may supply artefacts or images representing other solutions from other cultures. For example, in the rural areas of Ghana and Benin, West Africa, spherical clay pots are used to store water. The pots are unglazed and porous so that when standing in the shade and a draught they will keep water cool. Dry goods can also be kept in similar pots to protect them from insects. They stack perfectly on wide mouths so lids are not required (for further information on West African pottery see Loeb *et al.* 1993 and Courtney-Clarke 1990). By considering the local environment and sources of raw materials, children can better appreciate how such pots are an excellent use of available materials. The pots described have usually been constructed by hand using a traditional coiling technique. To make the larger pots with 2–3 litres' capacity requires a great deal of skill and dexterity. Children can be shown similar techniques and thus (thirdly) *discover their own creativity and competence as a basis for valuing the creativity and competence of others.*

If artefacts are presented in such a way that allows children to (fourthly) *come to understand the interaction of environmental needs and resources, techniques and cultural forms which leads to the creation of the forms of artefacts,* then any notions of primitive or underdeveloped technology might be replaced by wonder at the appropriate and economic use of materials, and recognition that the makers are skilled, patient and dexterous. The fifth key idea is for children *to begin to understand how cultural influences spread and interact*. This might be done by the examination of clothing of Hindu origin from northern India where embroidered and mirrored textiles are widespread. As well as examining the textiles in order to appreciate the skill of the maker and beauty of the items, the ways in which the motifs and materials used have been acquired by our Western fashion business could be highlighted by including some contemporary Western clothing employing similar techniques. This technology transfer has been happening since imports first arrived on our shores. For example, the Paisley design does not originate from Scotland, but from the stylised representation of a mango fruit on imported South Asian textiles. The origins of the moccasin slipper, anorak or pyjamas might also be researched. The attitude and approach of the teacher is of crucial importance, yet teachers will often feel that they have little knowledge of a particular culture. It is important that teachers are honest with their class about this and approach inquiry into other cultures in an open and questioning way. Teachers can only give children glimpses of what there is to know, but they can help them to come to realise there is so much more to find out about and begin to understand.

The following case study builds on aspects of the previous chapter in that it explores ways in which design and technology can be linked with music. The intention in this section is to show how these links can be used to foster an awareness and understanding of cultures in different times and places, while reinforcing the contribution music from other cultures makes to popular culture in the UK. The case study includes work that also addresses the citizenship dimension to the curriculum, a theme developed in more detail in Chapter 3.2.

Case Study 8 – Musical instruments (Year 5)

Introduction

This case study shows how the investigative, evaluative and research stages of a design and technology project can be used to emphasise our global interdependence. Western popular music has become increasingly influenced by the traditions of the east and south, and the rise in tourism has resulted in many homes containing examples of instruments from a variety of countries. The availability of world music CDs, CD-ROMS providing sound samples of instruments from around the world and information from the Internet has made it easier for children to find out about how instruments are made and used. Important points can be raised through such work about the innovative and enterprising use of resources by people with little money, the original and distinctive nature of the instruments and the differences between instruments made for the tourist market and those intended for serious music-making.

Setting the scene

Two Year 5 classes operate in parallel at Bromley Heath Junior School, South Gloucestershire. Richard White, design and technology subject leader, planned the musical instruments unit of work jointly with Alison Ayres, the other Year 5 teacher who is also science subject leader. Both classes had been looking at the life of John Lennon in the previous half term, so had been introduced to the Beatles' use of Indian instruments such as the sitar and tabla. The school is well resourced, with good Internet access for finding out about musical instruments around the world. Richard and Alison asked children to bring in examples from home, and supplemented these with those they had borrowed from a variety of sources. (Many LEAs, community groups and Development Education Centres have loan collections that schools can draw upon.)

Richard and Alison decided upon a focus for the project which included personal, social and health education (PSHE) and citizenship dimensions.

The teaching sequence

Richard introduced the topic by talking about his encounter with a musician and craftsman in India, whom he had met walking along a road playing a stringed instrument. When Richard had enquired about where he could buy one, the musician had given him the one he was playing.

Richard used this story to emphasise that many of the people who had made the instruments in the collection may have been poor materially, but were rich in other ways. He asked the children to think about the origins of music, and how it had come to be so important worldwide. Some of the children then spoke about the origins of the instruments they had brought in and the whole class considered the skilful use of materials and decoration in the collection.

Richard and Alison emphasised the need for care when handling, then distributed the instruments for investigation by pairs of children. They had provided a prompt sheet of questions to help children consider the design features of the instruments, but asked them to make notes initially rather than begin by answering the questions. Five minutes were allowed for making sounds with the instruments, then each pair was to look, feel and discuss their thoughts about the visual language of colours, symbols and patterns.

Some children considered the patterns on the maracas, and the arrangement of holes, which both reinforced the pattern and helped to let the sound out, while others looked closely at the arrangement of symbols on the steel drum, and decided that they were related to the pitch produced when different parts of the pan were hit. They also commented on the party atmosphere suggested by the painted decoration around the circumference.

A third group noticed how thin strips of leather had been twisted into spirals to tension the skins of the talking drum, producing both strength and a decorative effect (Fig. 2.4.1).

Figure 2.4.1 Evaluating a talking drum

In preparation for the second session, Richard and Alison asked the children to bring in any books or information about musical instruments that they had access to at home. During the lesson, children compiled information on a range of instruments from books, CD-ROMs and the Internet, helping them make decisions about the type of instrument they would like to make themselves.

Richard organised Internet access so that there were four children using the resource at any one time. He had previously logged onto two suitable websites; the children were instructed not to attempt access to any others, in order to protect them from unsuitable material. Access to the 'Musical Instruments' CD-ROM (Dorling Kindersley) was organised using the weekly computer rota, which involves pairs of children using the computer for approximately 20 minutes during morning break or lunchtime.

The children were surprised and amused by the range of musical instruments that they discovered through their research. They showed each other what they had found and soon started to see similarities between instruments which had very different origins geographically. They were intrigued by some of their findings and showed great enthusiasm for grouping instruments in families.

During the third session, the children started their FPT – making a sound box for their instrument. Ideas were discussed and Richard and Alison demonstrated how to cut 8mm-section wood safely using a hacksaw and a bench-hook. They showed the children how to construct a box using a card triangle technique (Williams and Jinks 1985) and offered them the choice between balsa and card as a sheet cladding material, depending upon the acoustic properties required. Richard and Alison felt that this activity would give everyone a starting point for the instrument they would go on to design (most instruments have sound boxes of some description) while offering them practice in key making skills.

It quickly became apparent that, although the children had used saws previously, they were not particularly proficient in their use by any means and much more teacher input was required than Richard had anticipated. Basic skills such as measuring lengths and holding wood while sawing needed practice. While building the frame children encountered problems trying to position the two sections of the box to be joined. They quickly discovered for themselves that working with a partner on this would be helpful.

The main differentiation strategy used during this unit of work came through additional support given to particular children who struggled with the making aspects of the project. Giving them the opportunity to help those having difficulties extended the skills of several more able pupils. Richard and Alison soon recognised that a one hour session to complete this aspect of the work would not be possible and so another hour was taken from the week's timetable to remedy this. They reflected later that small group work for this type of practical session, with the rest of the class involved in another activity, would have been more manageable and allowed them more time to spend with individuals, but timetable constraints meant that it was undertaken with the whole class.

The purpose of the fourth session was for the children to identify a form for their instrument and the context in which it would be used. Richard and Alison discussed with their classes the possibility of a performance to the rest of the school to put across an important citizenship-related social message. By taking a vote, the children agreed on the idea of raising awareness of poverty in countries of the 'Majority World' from which the instruments had come.

The next task for the children was to design some form of musical instrument by developing the sound box that most had already made. They had already discussed in previous sessions how different types of instruments are played by plucking, hitting, blowing, etc. and so had some idea of the type of instrument they were interested in making. The children's designs were mostly closely related to those they had investigated during the first session. Richard and Alison found it interesting that several of the children mentioned the importance of using inexpensive materials in their designs, in order to link with the theme of raising awareness of poverty. A purpose for their designing and making had been firmly established.

During sessions 5 and 6, Richard and Alison made a variety of tools and materials available to the children for the completion of their work. They were encouraged to select those most appropriate for their needs and guidance was given where necessary. Some children brought in additional resources from home for the completion of their work during week 6. These included such 'luxuries' as long elastic bands, silver foil, milk bottle tops and balloons (which were cut and stretched to give a small drum-skin effect).

When evaluating their instruments, children who stuck to their original plans seemed to gain satisfaction from the fact that their idea had worked out as they intended. Few seemed to want to improve upon their designs; those who did had quickly realised that aspects of their ideas were unrealistic and/or impractical. Richard and Alison noted that some of the children who did have to consider alternative methods found it difficult to come to terms with their initial failure and needed encouragement to reconsider their ideas. These were generally high-attaining children who had rarely encountered such challenges in their school work previously. It was an important lesson for them to accept help from others and develop attitudes of perseverance.

Richard and Alison had intended that by this stage the classes would be in a position to present an assembly to the rest of the school, showing their instruments and using them to put across the intended message relating to the problems of poverty in some countries of the world. In practice, the weeks leading up to Christmas did not allow time for adequate preparation for the intended outcome. However, the children were pleased to have been able to take a small part of a larger work-sharing assembly to perform a rap-style poem about world poverty, which was accompanied by musical instruments that they had designed and made.

Discussion

The children in Bromley Heath Junior School really enjoyed their work on musical instruments. They gained a much wider knowledge of the scope of instruments around the world, with some insight into how they had been made, from which materials and under what conditions. Through their research, they became more aware of diverse cultures and how these are often enriched by music and the instruments which make it. They developed skills in designing and making, becoming more informed in their selection of appropriate materials and tools, and more competent in their evaluating and decision-making. Through working together and realising that not everything goes to plan (and indeed that this is not always a bad thing!) the children gained a broader sense of achievement than in many other aspects of their work in school.

Further examples of work on musical instruments can be found in Ritchie (2001: case study 16) and Kane (1990), who provides a case study involving children in Key Stage 1 tackling a similar project. Other examples of projects involving collections of artefacts from other cultures include toys (QCA/DfEE 1998 Unit 5C), puppets (Unit 2B), clothes (including hats and shoes), building materials (Unit 1D) and cooking utensils. Collections of toys from around the world can fascinate children and lead to sophisticated discussions about who would play with them and who made them. Wire toys, such as model bicycles from South Africa, become even more impressive when the children discover that they are often made by the children themselves, using recycled materials. Trying to construct their own similar models can lead to enormous respect for the craft skills of the originators of the toys. However, Siraj-Blatchford (1996) cautions against undermining the value of such work by highlighting similarities with home-made toys played with by children's grandparents, which might reinforce stereotypical notions of backwardness.

Collections of artefacts from other cultures are often available locally through LEAs, Development Education Centres or for sale in fair trade outlets such as Oxfam. Increasingly, teachers are being given opportunities for educational visits overseas, which provide further opportunities for building up collections of artefacts. Ritchie (2001) provides the example of a teacher who had been to Mexico and brought back a collection of simple moving toys. The children evaluated these, produced exploded drawings and made their own versions. Again, respect for the original makers and insights into the innovative use of materials were important features of this project.

Work with foods is another area of design and technology where a multicultural approach is appropriate, as exemplified in the following case study.

Case Study 9 – Bread (QCA/DfEE 1998 Unit 5B Years 4, 5 and 6)

Introduction
This case study shows how a bread-making topic can help raise children's awareness of food from different cultures and the extent to which such foods have become part of their everyday experience.

Setting the scene
Sian Padget teaches a class of 38 children in Years 4, 5 and 6 at Old Sodbury Primary School, South Gloucestershire. In tackling the topic of bread, she decided to focus on it as a basic right of life, and address issues of global inequality in its distribution. Owing to a recent fuel dispute, there had been instances of panic buying of bread in the local supermarket, and Sian decided to look at greed and hoarding as part of the children's work towards the school's annual harvest festival celebrations. She also wanted to introduce children to a wide range of breads from around the world, and involve them in making decisions about the types of bread they would design and make. The curriculum objectives were taken from PSHE and citizenship (Key Stage 2) as well as design and technology.

The teaching sequence
Sian brought in a wide collection of types of bread, including pitta, ciabatta and sundried tomato bread. She asked the children as part of their evaluation to compile a product report, indicating their preferences.

In session 2, Sian asked the children to follow a recipe to make bread in order to develop their manual skills of kneading and shaping, but also to highlight the need for hygienic practices. The children drew up their design proposals for the specialist loaves in session 3, and gave Sian a list of ingredients which she brought in for the making session.

> The next session was devoted to making the bread, carried out as a whole-class activity in the hall. Two parent helpers were involved, and the children worked in groups of five or six to make up the basic dough. Their added ingredients were spread out centrally on a table. This enabled them to evaluate their earlier choices, and some made changes to their design in the light of the selection process.
>
> Children added their special ingredients carefully to the dough itself, or arranged them on the top. Once a wide range of outcomes had been produced, they were baked and tested, referring back to the original product analyses for comparison.

Discussion

Making bread is a fairly common design and technology task. Some significant strengths of Sian's approach were: the wide range of examples that she provided for the children to investigate and evaluate; the way in which the children produced product reports; and the planning for use of a wide range of additional ingredients. Its particular importance to our current discussion is the way in which Sian recognised the activity's potential for raising issues with children related to basic human needs and the way these are met in different parts of the world and by different cultural groups. The children's familiarity with most of the breads from their own home experiences reinforced their perception of the multicultural nature of their society, even in a predominantly white area.

Many food-related topics have similar potential. A useful QCA publication, *Food in Schools: Ideas* (1997), contains case studies illustrating this at Key Stages 1 and 2. One is entitled 'Indian contrasts' and features Year 6 children from a London primary school who visited two Indian restaurants to find out about the ingredients and techniques of Indian cooking (QCA 1997: 23–4). A project in Birmingham, initiated by the Birmingham Careers and Education Business Partnership, led to opportunities for primary school teachers to study, on placement, the significance of Balti food in the local community and economy. They produced curriculum materials to support teachers in organising visits to a spice importer, a sweet shop, restaurant, frozen food factory, fruit and vegetable shops and a wholesale market. Asking parents, particularly those from minority ethnic groups, to come into school and share their expertise and experiences is a good way of enriching children's learning when food is the medium being used for design and technology. Clearly, it is important for teachers to reinforce the message that the contribution of minority ethnic groups and other cultures to British society is not restricted to food.

Festivals and religious events provide good contexts for design and technology. Primary schools in this country increasingly celebrate a diverse range of festivals, such as Diwali, Eid, Hanukkah as well as more traditional Christian festivals such as Christmas and Easter. All such festivals have potential for design and technology activities – designing and making cards, presents and related artefacts (such as lamps for Diwali, the Hindu festival of light). The danger of a tokenistic approach needs to be addressed – the spiritual significance of light to Diwali needs to be an important focus of such work, rather than an excuse for some designing and making.

Many large cities around the country hold annual carnivals which can involve a diverse range of cultures and celebrate their differing traditions. Bristol has an annual St. Paul's carnival that attracts thousands to the streets for a celebration of Caribbean music, food and costume and also involves local schoolchildren in many ways. A carnival procession comprises floats and groups from schools. The children often wear costumes – some on a grand scale – that they have been involved in producing. At Sefton Park Junior School, members of St. Paul's community groups work with teachers and children in the weeks preceding the carnival to design and make their creations. The children learn various techniques for making wire frames and cladding them to create monsters or exotic insects depending on the chosen theme for the particular event.

Before leaving our discussion of multicultural education, there is one other approach we would like to highlight. The use of children's literature as a starting point for design and technology is common, as suggested in the previous chapter. Using design and technology friendly texts with a strong multicultural content is a way of taking this approach further. Examples with potential include: *Anancy and Mr Dry-Bone* by Fiona French (design and make something to make Miss Louisa laugh); *Emerald Blue* by Anne Marie Linden and Katherine Doyle (activities related to the hurricane and damage caused); and *Peter's Chair* by Ezra Jack Keats (design and make Peter a new chair). Such texts will increase the awareness and understanding of all children, especially those in schools where minority ethnic groups are not represented. For schools with a rich mix of cultures among pupils such texts are essential to ensure that all feel their background and home cultures are recognised and valued.

Anti-racist approaches to design and technology

While multicultural approaches to design and technology have been promoted throughout the life of the National Curriculum, an anti-racist perspective to design and technology is noticeable by its absence. This may be because anti-racism is seen as a political threat by the establishment for its critique of racist power structures within society (see Chapter 3.1). Anti-racist education recognises that it is necessary to challenge and oppose institutional racism in society and schools; in this it goes much further than multicultural approaches. Indeed, some would criticise multicultural education as tinkering with the curriculum while ignoring the major problem. While some advocates of anti-racism would dismiss multiculturalism, we see the two approaches as complementary and inextricably linked. The literature on anti-racist approaches to science education is well established (Dennick 1992; Gill and Levidov 1987); however there are relatively few references for design and technology.

The United Nations Educational, Scientific and Cultural Organisation (UNESCO), in its 1978 Declaration on Race and Prejudice, stated that racism includes 'racist ideologies, prejudiced attitudes, discriminatory behaviour, structural arrangements, and institutional practices resulting in racial inequality as well as the fallacious notion that discriminatory relations between groups are morally and scientifically justifiable' (UNESCO 1978). Does this have relevance to design and technology? Siraj-Blatchford (1994, 1996) claims that racism is reflected in aspects of the design and technology curriculum, although in the main it is recognised that it is the result of unintentional if uncritical application of culturally chauvinist attitudes:

> the notion of racial inequality is reproduced in, and through, ... design and technology education whenever an implied or explicit assumption of a First through Fourth World continuum of 'development', intellectual sophistication, or 'progress' is taken – that is, whenever we make the assumption that our 'developed' way of life is better than the life led by, for example, the indigenous communities of the Amazon rainforest or Kalahari desert. We can dispute the existence of any such continuum on the grounds of sustainability alone, and yet there is a deeper point to be made here. Science and technology education represent much more than just another valid sphere for anti-racist education. Science and technology lessons provide more than just one more context in which black children are disadvantaged and global inequalities sustained. Our treatment of science and technology in education and in the wider media has actually provided a major, if not

the major support to the most pervasive racist ideologies. Racism occurs when the application of prejudiced (albeit often unconscious or unintentional) attitudes lead to discriminatory actions. Many, if not most of the white ethnic majority population have grown up to believe themselves to be culturally (if not intellectually) superior to black people. Their 'common sense' (yet totally mistaken) everyday observations appear to confirm their prejudices: they see the relative poverty of Third and Fourth World communities in predominantly technological terms and they infer cultural (and individual) inferiority.

(Siraj-Blatchford and MacLeod-Brudenell 1999: 40)

This statement provides the rationale for those of us involved in design and technology to be proactive; not simply to promote the benefits to all of a multicultural society, but to use design and technology as one means to challenge implicit and explicit racist views. The case studies and examples given in the previous section provide potential for such approaches. An anti-racist teacher needs to be sensitive to the responses that pupils are making and be prepared to challenge those that are inappropriate. Such a teacher also has to be critical of texts and resources being used to ensure that they do not carry hidden messages about superiority or undervalue the achievements of those in the Majority World. Indeed, older children can be encouraged to question the terms 'Developing' or 'Third World' in order to highlight their inappropriateness. An anti-racist teacher will look for ways to promote the achievements and positive values of those from other ethnic groups. A good example of this was the way in which Richard White set the scene for the work on musical instruments with his account of meeting an Indian musician who happily gave him his instrument. Richard contrasted this man's apparent material poverty with his rich personal qualities and generosity. He also emphasised with the children the sophistication and skilled use of materials evident in the instruments.

One strategy that can be successfully adopted is to use case studies or biographies. There are numerous stories of the technological achievements of black women and men that can be used to challenge notions of the superiority of white Western culture and achievement. A classic example is the case of Charles Drew (1904–1950) who perfected a way of storing blood during the Second World War. The Red Cross set up the first blood transfusion unit using his work. In 1948 he was made a professor in recognition of his achievements. Two years later he was involved in a serious car crash near a hospital in Alabama, where segregation of whites and blacks was rigid. Drew was refused entry to the white hospital which had a blood transfusion unit; he later died from blood loss. His ideas are employed by all transfusion services and have saved many lives. Sharing such a story with older primary pupils can be used as a starting point for discussions about racism and the achievement of black scientists and technologists.

Another often-cited example relates to the invention of the electric light bulb – usually attributed to the white American Thomas Edison. In fact, the first person to obtain a patent was Lewis Latimer, an African-American. He also prepared all the technical documentation for Alexander Bell's patent for the telephone. Children may be familiar with the phrase the 'real McCoy'. They probably will not know that it refers to Elizah McCoy (1843–1929), the son of slaves, who invented a self-lubricating unit for the axles of trains while employed as a maintenance engineer on the American railroads. The device was so popular that soon all locomotives carried the system. Potential buyers began to ask if the lubrication system for the axles was a 'real McCoy' and hence the phrase was born. Such examples, which are interesting stories in their own right, have the potential to challenge children's attitudes towards, and understanding of, technology. They are part of the way we can put technology in its place. Similar distortions of history apply to the place of women in science and technology, which have been challenged through anti-sexist approaches (e.g. Browne 1991).

Teachers may also find materials from the charity Intermediate Technology useful in identifying ways in which they can promote anti-racism through the design and technology curriculum. This international development agency has offices in Sri Lanka, Bangladesh, Nepal, Sudan, Kenya and Zimbabwe that work in partnership with communities to facilitate appropriate technology choices. The staff of the education unit are keen to work with educators who wish to integrate the teaching of appropriate technology, global and development issues in their curriculum planning. The agency produces a range of curriculum support materials that are piloted by practising teachers. The materials are designed to:

> challenge racist and ethnocentric stereotypes; develop students' global awareness; stimulate students' thinking and critical awareness; introduce students to the resourcefulness and inventiveness that exists all over the world; give students the sense of being participators in, not merely observers of, our world and increase understanding of the wider issues related to technology.
>
> (Hammond 1997: 53)

An essential aspect of their approach is to show parallels between the technological products and processes in the UK and elsewhere within a social, environmental and cultural context, while at the same time appreciating differences and the reasons for them (for example, in the packaging of food products). Another dimension to this approach is to consider the historical context within which technologies have developed, to which we turn next.

Approaching design and technology through historical contexts

We have discussed design and technology involving artefacts and food in terms of the contribution made to children's understanding of different cultures and their traditions. The same approach can be easily adopted to educating children about the technology of other times, which has a different contribution to make to children's cultural education. Collections of artefacts from other periods of history can be compared and contrasted with our own, offering another perspective through which children can understand their own lives and technology's contribution to them. A comparative activity could be set up as an IEA, using, for example, a Victorian board game and a high tech games console which could lead to interesting discussion about values and social behaviours.

The education staff at the Museum of London developed a handling collection of 'light sources through the ages'. The collection included a Roman oil lamp, Victorian lanterns, early electric torches used by the police and hooded lamps for use during wartime blackouts. The learning materials accompanying the collection invited children to consider the specific circumstances in which they were used and list special design features. This led to school projects involving children in designing their own lighting for a specific historical period (using materials and fuels that would have been available). A useful publication giving guidance on observing and developing curriculum work from historical artefacts is *A Teacher's Guide to Learning from Objects* (Durbin *et al.* 1990).

For children in schools near Roman sites, a trip to view baths, hypocausts and other Roman plumbing for comparison with modern municipal facilities or modern plumbing has similar potential. While increasing children's understanding and awareness of technologies in other times is not strictly a multicultural issue, it does have a contribution to make to children's cultural education which has some parallels. For example, it encourages children to question their own values and approach to everyday life in new ways by comparison with those of others. Ritchie (2001) discusses other examples of this, including children whose understanding of their grandparents' wartime experiences was increased through a project in which they designed and made model air-raid shelters. The cultural aspects of this project related to interviews with grandparents about their memories and finding out about how time was spent in the shelters: learning to sing songs and play games from that period. Solomon (1995) provides some helpful materials including stories from history to be used in teaching technology.

Design and technology linked to learning about other countries

Topics with a focus on a particular country provide another starting point and context for design and technology. Seberry (1996) provides a case study in which children found out about Japanese culture and traditions, learning how to make lanterns and about calligraphy. Ritchie (2001) offers an example where children's learning about Italy was enriched by them setting up an Italian restaurant.

International linking between schools, especially through the use of ICT and email, provides excellent opportunities for children to design and make presents or artefacts for each other – even if only through a digital photograph sent as an email attachment (see Chapters 2.1 and 2.3). An example from a Bristol school involved a novel idea in which children in a Year 5 class had to select artefacts that were important in their daily lives to send to a partner school, but they were restricted to a shoe box. This led to discussions about what to include and why. They were keen to ensure a mix of low and high technology, drawn from their leisure as well as school lives. 'Travel buddies' are increasingly promoted through European initiatives such as those funded through European Commission (EC) grants (Comenius Projects). Travel buddies are usually soft toys that are circulated around partner schools in different countries. After one such Comenius course based in Bath, a teddy bear called Newton visited eight countries in a year, 'sending' information and resources to partner schools from the country in which he was being hosted. These exchanges included information about, for example, favourite foods and games. A future proposal is for him to be dressed by children in both traditional costume and in contemporary fashion for the country involved. Newton carried with him a passport and travel journal, including photographs, recording his journey around Europe. Another travel buddy recently left Luckwell, Bristol with a head teacher on an exchange visit to Mozambique (where the city of Bera is twinned with Bristol). This lion returned with lots of resources, such as musical instruments, pictures and stories to 'tell' of life with children in Mozambique. The potential for design and technology activities based on such resources and information is considerable; for example children could design and make luggage for the travel buddy to carry their presents in.

Summary

This chapter has addressed the third strand of cultural education and understanding discussed in Chapter 2.1: the interaction between different cultural forms and traditions. It has provided some examples of the following roles for design and technology education in the cultural development of young people:

- to enable young people to recognise, explore and understand their own cultural assumptions and values;

- to enable young people to embrace and understand cultural diversity by bringing them into contact with the attitudes, values and traditions of others;

- to encourage an historical perspective by relating contemporary values to the processes and events that have shaped them;

- to enable young people to understand the evolutionary nature of culture and the processes and potential for change.

(NACCCE 1999: 48)

Additionally, the links between multicultural education and anti-racist approaches have been discussed and the importance of the latter in contemporary society emphasised.

This section of the book has focused on ways in which design and technology education can contribute to children's cultural awareness, understanding and apprenticeship. It has been structured around the three strands identified in *All Our Futures* (NACCCE 1999: 42): the cultural impact of science and technology; the relationship between the arts, technology and design; and the interaction between different cultural forms and traditions. In all of these strands, teachers' creativity in identifying appropriate opportunities to enhance children's learning in design and technology has been illustrated together with children's creative responses to those opportunities. In both areas we have sought to build on the creative foundations established in Section One. In the next section we will explore how children can use their creativity and cultural understanding to begin to contribute to the future of the society in which they live.

Citizenship education through design and technology contexts

Why citizenship?

Purpose of this chapter

Through reading this chapter you will gain:

- an understanding of different meanings of citizenship education and the political traditions from which they derive

- an insight into the close relationship between design and technology and citizenship in the primary curriculum

- strategies for involving children in citizenship at different levels through design and technology activities.

Introduction

In Chapter 2.1 we described the multiple and overlapping cultures to which children belong – family, school, team, religious group, society, global village etc. They are *members* of such groups by being themselves (i.e. without trying), yet there is a further level of *active participation* in the structures which surround them – that of *citizenship*. There are probably as many meanings of the word 'citizenship' as 'culture', yet for the purpose of this book we choose to define one in terms of the other. Citizenship can be thought of as culture with a political dimension. It is about exercising certain rights and responsibilities within the institutions which surround us: our homes, places of work, voluntary organisations and clubs, local and national government, global power structures. Citizenship may well be about working *within* these dominant cultures, but equally it may *challenge* the assumptions underlying them.

Of course, many groups in society (particularly children) are excluded from the political participation implied by being a citizen. Indeed, they may not recognise the *legitimacy* of the state and its instruments (police, social workers etc.), having suffered at its hands. The state may be seen as the enemy and citizenship of such a state as having no meaning. For this reason we must be sensitive in dealing with this emotive issue in the classroom. It would perhaps be better to see the aims of citizenship education as *emancipatory* and *empowering,* i.e. helping children to take control of their lives and the things that matter to them, rather than as part of their responsibility to society. In this respect it shares many of the ideals of design and technology, which aims to help children believe they can change things for the better.

These aims are reflected in recent National Curriculum documentation, which defines citizenship education as giving pupils the 'knowledge, skills and understanding to play an effective role in society at local, national and international levels' (DfEE/QCA 1999b: 12). Although non-statutory at Key Stages 1 and 2, the recent publication of guidelines for citizenship at primary level within the framework of PSHE signals the government's commitment to enhancing its status in primary schools. This section of the book will look at the contribution of design and technology to citizenship education through its promotion of technological and visual literacy, fostering of key skills and potential for building sustainable futures.

But what kind of citizenship are we talking about? For some, the whole notion of citizenship is alien to UK political tradition (Crawford 1999), since Britain is a monarchy without a written constitution. They might argue that the British are subjects rather than citizens, and ask the question: 'How can there be real citizenship without real democracy?' This view is probably in the minority however; Dixon (1999) has estimated that there are currently around 200 organisations with an active interest in citizenship education. Between them, they represent very different interpretations of what it means to be a citizen. Dixon has grouped these interpretations under the following three headings, deriving from different historical and political perspectives.

The 'classical' tradition

Citizenship education needs to start from the values and associated institutional practices and civic virtues of liberal democracy.

(White 1999: 59)

The classical tradition of citizenship is the Graeco-Roman one in which 'those deemed to be citizens, women and slaves being excluded, had not only the right but the obligation to take part in civic life' (Dixon 1999: 2). Such a preoccupation with democratic duty has driven countries such as Australia to make voting compulsory, and has influenced several citizenship education initiatives in the UK, such as the Hansard Society report of 1978, *Political Education and Political Literacy*. The early (and much neglected) version of citizenship as a cross-curricular theme in the National Curriculum (NCC 1990b) drew upon such a perspective, as did the establishment in 1996 by the Schools Curriculum and Assessment Authority of the National Forum for Values in Education and the Community, which had as its aim 'understanding our responsibilities as citizens in society'. Even the recent Crick Report (QCA 1998) can be seen to derive some of its key principles from this republican model: social and moral responsibility, community involvement and political literacy.

Such a view of citizenship (much favoured by politicians) tends to lead to the teaching of 'civics' – facts about institutions, respectable fantasies about the universal good work of elected representatives both local and national – and has as one of its core values the respect of individuals for the state and existing power structures. It is an inherently conservative model, with emphasis upon knowledge, passivity and order within society, i.e. maintaining the *status quo*. The term *minimalist* has been used to characterise this formal, legal approach. Unsurprisingly, such a perspective has attracted considerable criticism for its patrician overtones: 'If it is presented in a finger-wagging, dry way, then Citizenship Education is doomed' (Supple 1999: 16).

Our experience and belief is that children will simply not be engaged or enthused by such an approach. They need a citizenship education which is 'relevant to all the school population, (drawing) from concepts that children actually hold or that are at least familiar to them' (Crick 1999: 342) and helping children to develop these embryo ideas (of fairness or sharing for example) into principles that will inform their understanding of society. The real-life scenarios and joint decision-taking potential within design and technology activity can provide just the starting points that children need to gain a sense of democratic participation, for example in establishing shared safety rules or voting on the name of a product to improve life for a member of the local community. Design and technology is not about accepting what already exists. Designers must be *future-oriented* and, while learning from past products and systems, need to break with conventional solutions rather than replicate them. So a citizenship education based on respect for existing structures and authorities will have less to offer children than other more transforming models such as those below.

The 'liberal-democratic' tradition

In England, the liberal-democratic tradition dates back to the 17th century (the time of the English revolution) and because of its birth in the unrest of the disenfranchised, tends to emphasise citizen's *rights* above their *responsibilities*. Such a model has strong support from the left of the political spectrum, and is primarily concerned with issues such as *social justice*: 'Citizenship education provides an opportunity for young people to see justice as everyone's business' (Supple 1999: 18).

This version of citizenship is particularly concerned with the participation of traditionally disadvantaged and excluded groups, such as women and black people. Feminist and anti-racist versions of citizenship education have emerged in recent years, with the aim of shifting children's perceptions of society in order to make it more just in the future. These perspectives question the way in which the notion of a citizen assumes a white male status within society, ignoring the power relationships that disenfranchise oppressed groups. For example, Arnot and Dillabough (2000) maintain that feminist citizenship needs to confront the divide between the public (traditionally male) and private (traditionally female) spheres of life. Similarly, Gilroy (1986), in *There Ain't No Black in the Union Jack*, criticises the assumption that the inclusive 'we' of citizenship covers all groups within society, when many do not share the same allegiances and representation.

Some curricular materials have begun to address these issues. For example, the Citizenship Foundation published materials for the primary school in 1994, entitled *You, Me and Us!*, which had as its aims 'fostering a predisposition to justice, a positive view of cultural diversity and building a community of the classroom' (Supple 1999: 17). Such a perspective has clearly influenced the Blair government, which cited citizenship education as an important factor in promoting racial harmony following the Stephen Lawrence enquiry and other examples of xenophobia such as the behaviour of English football fans abroad (Osler 1999). However, anti-racist citizenship is not a strong feature of the Crick Report, which tends to emphasise assimilation of minority groups within the dominant political culture: 'Minorities must learn and respect the laws, codes and conventions as much as the majority' (QCA 1998: 10).

Such a statement could be taken to imply that minorities have different codes and conventions from the majority, or that they are more likely to break them (Appiah 1999). It leaves itself open to a racist interpretation. A better approach perhaps would be to emphasise the shared beliefs and values of people with diverse backgrounds, so that the citizenship curriculum builds mutual understanding and shared purpose:

> Society can sustain lifestyle differences and cultural differences for example, but to be in a state of equilibrium it needs common values, goals and interests. The citizenship curriculum ... can make a significant contribution to fostering such commonality in multicultural Britain.
>
> (Appiah 1999: 23)

The extent to which this is achievable is open to debate – for some the very notion of shared values within a national identity undermines the rights of minorities. In a diverse, multicultural, pluralistic society such as contemporary Britain, is a common citizenship desirable or achievable (Crawford 1999: 120)? Nevertheless, design and technology, with its emphasis upon human needs and values, can have a role to play in building shared understandings between children from different backgrounds. Chapter 2.4 considers what anti-racist design and technology education might look like in practice, using stories of technological developments in different cultures. Layton (1992) points to the problems of *technology transfer* – implementing solutions in situations very different from those for which the technology was originally designed. He cites the introduction of snowmobiles in Lapland, the outlay and maintenance that rendered them unaffordable by all but the largest herd owners, thus forcing many out of business. Similar stories of technology benefiting the powerful and driving the small business 'to the wall' could be told in agricultural and retail settings throughout the world. Children in upper primary (ages seven upwards) are capable of identifying the winners, losers and injustices in such examples.

For some teachers, the liberal-democratic model of citizenship education is too radical and underemphasises the preparation of children to function in society *as it is*, rather than as we would like it to become (for others it is not radical enough!). Perhaps there is a need to find a balance between rights and responsibilities, to help children understand their relationship to authority in its different forms – parents, teachers, government etc. – rather than to challenge it continually. As one of those authorities, it is presumably in the teacher's interests to encourage respect as well as a questioning attitude in children. The third of our three models for citizenship offers this third way, one of active participation within existing structures to make changes for the better.

The 'liberal-republican' model

For many years, concepts of citizenship have been polarised between the positions described above, yet there is increasing evidence of a new tradition, born out of the other two and emanating from the United States – a liberal-republican model, which:

> while emphasising the rights of the individual, also stresses that individuals have a duty towards the needs of the community and by so doing they are then perceived to earn the right to be considered a citizen by way of this active involvement.

(Dixon 1999: 4)

With this has come the notion of active citizenship, which is not confined to voting and volunteering but implies a sense of care about important issues and the willingness to use democratic channels to make our voices heard. For example, the notion of Green citizenship implies an active concern for our local and global environment, centred around Agenda 21 from the Rio Earth Summit of 1992: 'In essence, Agenda 21 is about taking action locally to help resolve global problems' (Bloomfield 1998: 97).

Within the framework of Agenda 21 lies the concept of sustainability, which is a key issue that needs to be incorporated into children's designing and making. They need to see themselves as global citizens, taking local decisions that will affect future generations. In practice, much good work is already being carried out in schools, including litter collection and recycling (see Chapter 2.2). According to Bloomfield (1998) however, such activities are not enough in themselves; children must begin to examine the underlying issues. Why is food sold with so much card, cellophane and polystyrene packaging? Is it really to protect our health or to make the product look attractive on the supermarket shelves? Chapter 3.4 deals with the design and technology implications of a liberal-republican model in more depth, but in the meantime we need to consider the different levels at which children can participate in their society and culture.

Citizens of the school

The most obvious forum where children can exercise active citizenship is their school, since alone of the various subcultures to which they belong it is a formal *institution*:

> The school, while not entirely a 'microcosm' of society, nonetheless replicates certain features of power and control ... (children) should begin with positioning their own experience of institutional life, to establish whether and how it matches other institutions in our 'democratic' society.
>
> (Davies 1999: 40)

Furthermore, it is the institution through which successive governments have sought to induct children into the dominant notions of society concerning 'right' and 'wrong'. The problems of disaffected youth, rising crime and social disintegration have often been blamed on schools for failing to give moral leadership. Schools tend to respond to this criticism by claiming that values such as respect, tolerance and care for others permeate the ethos of everything that goes on within them, being part of the hidden curriculum imparted through teachers' words and actions. One of the purposes behind the introduction of citizenship education is to make these implicit messages explicit while ensuring that clearer moral guidance is given to children. A consequence of this could be the tendency to *accentuate* the teacher–pupil power relationship. For ultimately, even within an area of the curriculum such as design and technology where children are given choices about materials and outcomes, the teacher is in charge (usually!) and makes the final decisions.

Given the reality of power in the classroom, are children really citizens of the school in anything more than name, or could the term 'subjects' be more accurately applied to them? Davies (1999) suggests several ways in which children's perceptions of being school citizens might be explored, including *power maps*: asking the children to draw a rough map of the school, using coloured stickers to show the places where important decisions are made or where the powerful people are. Another approach is by asking the question 'What if you want to change something?' 'Small scenarios which presented a problem needing change invited children's suggestions for how it might be done' (Davies 1999: 41). Both of these activities could be used as part of a design and technology project, since the power map could involve elements of planning and graphic presentation, while changing an aspect of the school environment is an often-used design brief for DMAs. For example, Unit 2B in the National Scheme of Work for Key Stages 1 and 2 (QCA/DfEE 1998) invites children to design new playground play equipment.

All schools have a governing body that will include some parents, but some take the notion of participatory democracy a stage further through a school council with elected pupil representatives. These can take decisions with a design and technology dimension. For example, the QCA National Scheme of Work for Citizenship at Key Stages 1 and 2 (QCA/DfEE 2001) makes several suggestions for activities that school and class councils can be involved in, for example fundraising for improvements to the school playground, and devising new playground games. Designing and making a game with instructions is a much used and often highly successful DMA, involving children in real evaluation and modification in the light of experience. Linking this activity to the work of a school or class council can add an extra motivating dimension for children. Further ideas can be found in the *Primary School Councils Toolkit* (Schools Councils UK).

With positive early experiences of participating in an institution such as school, children are far more likely to feel that their voices can be heard at local, district and national levels. The research of Schweinhart and Weikart (1997) in the United States indicated that children with positive early experiences of school, including a curriculum emphasising citizenship values, were three times more likely to participate fully in society in later life than those experiencing a narrow subject-based early childhood education. In a context in which many of the 'English' feel confused about their national identity (because of devolution and the growth of European government) such early experiences are an essential prerequisite to gaining a sense of identity through active citizenship. It is however also important that children begin to see themselves as part of broader transnational groups.

Citizens of the world

Relating closely to a liberal-republican model of citizenship – linked to sustainability and Agenda 21 (see Chapter 3.4) – the field of *global education* is one with a well-established set of principles (Hicks 1999). Developing *global citizenship* education involves questioning our assumptions about the model of citizenship that we seek to foster:

> Notions of citizenship are not neutral for they embody the value judgements of their creators ... There is thus a danger that in discussing the importance of citizenship western concepts are taken to be universal ones.
>
> (Hicks 1999: 15)

Oxfam (1997) have defined a curriculum for global citizenship, with the strands and principles shown in Table 3.1.1.

Knowledge and understanding	Skills	Values and attitudes
Social justice and equity Peace and conflict Globalisation and interdependence Cultural diversity Sustainable development	Cooperation and conflict-resolution Critical thinking Ability to argue effectively Ability to challenge injustice and inequality	Sense of identity and self-esteem Empathy Value and respect for diversity Commitment to social justice and equity Concern for environment and sustainable development Belief that people can make a difference

Source: Oxfam (1997)

Table 3.1.1 Principal components of a curriculum for global citizenship

Of the skills domain in Table 3.1.1, those such as 'cooperation' and 'critical thinking' could clearly be developed through design and technology activity, while many of the knowledge and values aspects could be included within the brief for projects, or drawn out by skilful questioning by the teacher while children are working. For example, a project to design a bicycle trailer for use in rural India (Mulberg 1992) drew upon the research of the Intermediate Technology Group into locally available materials and techniques, thus reducing the reliance on Western technology for transporting goods. The children learnt about the villages in which the trailer would be used, developing a respect for diversity and relating the challenges faced by Indian villagers to their own needs to move around and carry things safely. Such local initiatives need to be set within a broader framework, which recognises the power of globalisation to move capital around the world through transnational corporations, relocating to regions with cheap labour and little regulation. Educational materials on globalisation are produced by Teachers in Development Education (TIDE).

Citizenship in the National Curriculum

Despite the empowering potential of citizenship education within the liberal-republican model, research indicates that primary teachers are either unaware of it or see it as a burden (Supple 1999). Many see it purely in terms of personal qualities to be developed in children, i.e. that we should educate young children to be good, moral people, but any political dimension should come much later. Given this weak foundation, the architects of the National Curriculum opted to make citizenship education non-statutory at Key Stages 1 and 2, preferring to include it within a broader PSHE framework. This framework comprises the following sections:

- Developing confidence and responsibility and making the most of their abilities
- Preparing to play an active role as citizens
- Developing a healthy, safer lifestyle

Clearly, only the second of these three headings is explicitly citizenship-related, although the others can be seen as laying down some of the basic life-skills and establishing a positive self-image, which will help give children the confidence to be active citizens. Although several cross-curricular links are indicated in the Programme of Study margin – including links with design and technology – these are largely restricted to the 'healthy, safer lifestyle' section; for example the safe use of tools. There is much more to the citizenship potential of design and technology than this!

Progression in citizenship education within the National Curriculum

The introduction to the Programme of Study (PoS) for PSHE and citizenship at Key Stage 1 makes it clear that for young children the emphasis is upon their immediate social surroundings:

> As members of a class and school community, they learn social skills such as how to share, take turns, play, help others, resolve simple arguments and resist bullying. They begin to take an active part in the life of their school and its neighbourhood.
>
> (DfEE/QCA 1999b: 137)

Examples at this level include the opportunity to take part in discussions, make real choices and meet with people from the community, in order to 'recognise the difference between right and wrong', and see themselves as belonging to 'various groups and communities, such as family and school'.

By Key Stage 2, the scope of the requirements becomes much broader, with the introduction of a national and international perspective, together with the opportunity for children to develop and reflect upon a wider set of values underpinning their role as citizens:

They learn about the wider world and the interdependence of communities within it. They develop their sense of social justice and moral responsibility and begin to understand that their own choices and behaviour can affect local, national or global issues and political and social institutions.

(DfEE/QCA 1999b: 139)

The programmes of study for this age group are correspondingly more complex and demanding, with the requirements to 'research, discuss and debate topical issues, problems and events' and to 'participate' (for example, in the school's decision-making process, relating it to democratic structures and processes such as councils, parliaments, government and voting). Such activities, it is claimed, will give children an understanding of 'what democracy is, and about the basic institutions that support it locally and nationally', together with an appreciation that rules and values may be in conflict in different situations, and that distribution of wealth and resources 'affect individuals, communities and the sustainability of the environment'.

Design and technology as citizenship education

There is to date little published work on citizenship within design and technology yet the two subjects share striking similarities. Let us examine the 'Importance of Design and Technology' statement from the National Curriculum:

Design and technology prepares pupils to participate in tomorrow's rapidly changing technologies. They learn to think and intervene creatively to improve quality of life. The subject calls for pupils to become autonomous and creative problem solvers, as individuals and members of a team. They must look for needs, wants and opportunities and respond to them by developing a range of ideas and making products and systems. They combine practical skills with an understanding of aesthetics, social and environmental issues, function and industrial practices. As they do so, they reflect on and evaluate present and past design and technology, its uses and effects. Through design and technology, all pupils can become discriminating and informed users of products, and become innovators.

(DfEE/QCA 1999a: 15)

Practically every sentence of this rationale is explicitly citizenship-related. For example, in order to become 'informed citizens' in a technological age, children need the 'technological literacy' to 'read' the products around them. This occurs on the level of functionality (line 7) and consumerism – becoming 'discriminating and informed users of products' (line 10) – but also at deeper societal levels: 'understanding of ... social and environmental issues ... uses and effects' (lines 7–9).

Design and technology self-evidently develops 'skills of enquiry and communication', for example in seeking out 'needs, wants and opportunities' (lines 4–5) and in going on to develop 'a range of ideas' (line 5) and solve problems (line 4). That these skills should be developed as 'part of a team' (line 4) necessitates effective communication.

Design and technology activity cannot take place without 'participation and responsible action', since to 'intervene creatively to improve quality of life' (lines 2–3) requires that children participate in 'communities' at different levels to experience quality of life and learn what the members of each community require to improve it.

It may be no exaggeration to claim that design and technology *is* citizenship education. Other subjects may claim strong links (for example geography or religious education) but we would argue that just as it has a double helping of creativity (see Chapter 1.1), design and technology should be seen as one of the primary vehicles for citizenship education. This is one way in which it can retain a foothold or even enhance its status in the primary curriculum, but to achieve this requires creative rather than merely effective teaching.

The remaining chapters in this section will explore ways in which we can teach the citizenship strands identified in Curriculum 2000 (above) by placing them in a specifically design and technological context. In Chapter 3.2 we consider the contribution that design and technology can make to children becoming informed citizens. We offer strategies for developing design and technological awareness in primary-age children, enabling them to understand how products come to be as they are, and also to question the direction of technological development. Chapter 3.3 considers how the skills of enquiry and communication that children can develop through design and technology may be transferred to their citizenship education.

In Chapter 3.4 we deal in greater depth with the issues of active citizenship, such as those involved in creating sustainable futures through participation at the levels of school, community, society and world. This is where design and technology activities can play their most significant role in contributing to children's citizenship education, while acknowledging that the relationship is a reciprocal one, where the real decisions of citizens can bring added dimensions to otherwise artificial design briefs.

Summary

In this chapter we have introduced our definition of citizenship, as 'culture with a political dimension', involving children in participation within – and sometimes challenging – the cultures and institutions of which they are a part. We have explored the models of citizenship education recommended in the Crick Report (QCA 1998) and subsequently enshrined in the National Curriculum (DfEE/QCA 1999b) against three alternative versions derived from differing assumptions about the relationship between the individual and society. Most importantly, this chapter has asserted the fundamental connections between design and technology education and citizenship, drawing upon a range of examples in which children have taken steps to get involved in their school, community and wider world in order to improve the lives of themselves and others. In this respect it has set the scene for the chapters to come, which develop this relationship in more detail and offer guidelines for teaching citizenship through design and technology activities.

Becoming informed citizens through design and technology

Purpose of this chapter

Through reading this chapter you will gain:

- an understanding of the relationship between capability and awareness in design and technology education

- an appreciation of the contribution that design and technological awareness can make to citizenship education

- an awareness of the wider areas of knowledge and understanding children need to become informed citizens.

Introduction

Citizenship is such a multidimensional construct that a number of areas will require preparatory work, as acknowledged by placing it within the context of PSHE at Key Stages 1 and 2 in the National Curriculum. This chapter explores some of these areas in depth, but does so in the context of children's awareness, which must underpin the skills they develop (Chapter 3.3) and the actions they take (Chapter 3.4). We start with what we believe to be an essential component of understanding citizenship in a post-industrial, 21st-century society: that of *technological literacy*.

There are two major strands in design and technology education: the development of *capability* (children working through a design process to develop new products) and the fostering of design and technological *awareness* (making sense of the made world). The first of these involves the development of mainly *procedural* knowledge (identifying needs, planning for making etc.) whereas the second is largely concerned with *conceptual* knowledge (about materials, processes, finishes, costs etc.). Permeating both is the strong *attitudinal* dimension of design and technology, which being a subject concerned with human aspiration involves *value judgements* by children at every stage (see Chapter 2.1) concerned with a wider notion of cost (for example ethical and environmental). This is in some ways an artificial separation of a *holistic* activity, since children's development of design and technology capability will inevitably draw upon their understanding at each stage, and an important part of their awareness will concern the processes used by designers and technologists to create the products around them. However, for the purposes of becoming informed citizens it is this awareness strand that concerns us most, since children's understanding of the decisions taken by designers and technologists enables them to make informed choices as consumers and contribute to debates concerning the direction of new technological developments. One important aspect of this strand has been described as *technological literacy* – the ability to 'read' manufactured products and appreciate their wider significance.

Technological literacy

> It is a myth that teaching *about* technology is the same as teaching how to *live in* a technological society.
>
> (Mulberg 1992: 31)

As a society we are faced with increasingly complex decisions about which technologies to adopt, which to discard and which to actively rebel against. Who controls the direction of technological development? Do we as citizens ever have a say, and if so do we have access to the information on which to base an informed decision? In the rapidly expanding field of biotechnology, ethical issues seem to arise every day. Some citizens, having arrived at an assessment of the balance of pros and cons for GM crops, choose to take direct action and destroy field trials. Yet agriculturalists in several African, Central American and Asian countries point to the vast potential of such disease-resistant high-yield seeds for feeding fast-expanding populations. Who is right?

Today's children will need to engage in such technological decision-making with increasing frequency, both as individuals and as members of pressure groups within society as a whole. They need crucially to have available not only the technological information they need, but also the tools in order to evaluate such information – which in the context of written language would be termed literacy skills. Hence we derive the concept of technological literacy, which Rennie and Jarvis (1994: 5) define in the following terms:

> Becoming technologically literate means becoming informed and knowledgeable about technological products and processes. If we are informed, we can select carefully and be safe users of the products and processes we need. If we learn more about technology, it will help us feel less threatened by how quickly things change and the bewildering range of new products we see.

Rennie and Jarvis' definition above relates principally to the role of the consumer, which children adopt at an early age with increasing sophistication. It is only necessary to watch Saturday morning commercial television to see the ways in which their spending power is targeted by advertisers. Advertisers admit as much, and have a term – 'tweenagers' – for the target consumer group of primary-age children who are influenced by popular culture. They are generally quicker to assimilate new products than adults, but lack a wider understanding of the impact of such technologies upon themselves and others. Hence Benyon and Mackay (1992: 22) have broadened the concept of technological literacy to include a social and political dimension, which relates it more closely to notions of citizenship:

> In my view, understanding technology … implies far more than just 'knowing' about some of its social effects. It means being able to 'read it' … technologies are not neutral objects but rather 'historical-social projects' with in-built 'social constituents' to serve ruling interests … Being able to 'read' technology is being able to tease out these ideological aspects and recognise their origins and implications.

Although it may be unrealistic for primary-age children to engage with the ideological aspects of technology, they can begin to develop the ability to read it through IEAs (DfEE/QCA 1999a) in which they not only consider how products work, but think about the ways in which people might use them.

Developing children's technological literacy

Part of this process may be getting children to think about how technology has changed in the past and is changing now. For example, the Design Museum in London's Docklands has loan collections of household goods (telephones, electric kettles etc.) showing the evolution of designs for such appliances over time. Children asking their grandparents for old examples of a particular product from their attics would be an alternative way of resourcing such activities. A set of questions for evaluation might include the following:

- How have the shapes (sizes, colours, materials, features) of this product changed over time?

- What could some of the reasons for this be (new materials, changes in fashion, new functions for the product, different target users)?

- Why do you think the designers of these products feel that they have to keep changing them (competition in the market place, desire for new things)? What would happen if the product just stayed the same?

- Are there any problems with constant change (replacement rather than repair, people throw away things that work because they're old-fashioned)?

A useful introduction to developing children's technological literacy through product evaluation is provided by DfEE (1995) *Looking at Values through Products and Applications*. This publication includes the example of a collection of T-shirts, which has the added advantage of conveying an explicit message through graphic media, thus offering opportunities for developing visual as well as technological literacy (see Chapter 1.3). An IEA of this type could be used as part of Unit 2D ('Joseph's coat') in the National Scheme of Work for Design and Technology (QCA/DfEE 1998). T-shirts are produced by organisations with direct involvement in global citizenship issues (Greenpeace, Oxfam etc.), which can further enhance the discussion that comes through evaluating them. The example used by DfEE (1995) was produced in Zimbabwe by Design Inc. and marketed through the UK charity Traidcraft, which purchases fairly traded goods in the Majority World, while offering partner companies design and business support. The evaluative questions suggested are as follows:

- Does this T-shirt appeal to you?

- Is it because of the policies of Design Inc. and Traidcraft?

- Is it because you like the design?

- What sort of person do you think would buy this T-shirt?

- Would it be for personal use or as a gift?

- Would you rather support environmental and world health projects in this way, or by giving direct to charity?

If this activity were to lead into a DMA, children could make use of ICT to design their T-shirt logo (or the pattern for Joseph's coat), printing directly onto newly available fabric transfer sheets for ink-jet printers. There is, of course, a wide range of other issues children could be asked to explore through evaluating T-shirts. These include such cross-curricular dimensions as the *spiritual* (many T-shirt motifs have a spiritual content, Traidcraft is a Christian organisation); *moral* (the difference between fair and unfair trade); *social* (Who are the workers at Design Inc.? How are they linked to us, the consumers?) and *economic* (How much does it cost? Where do the profits go?). The industrial emphasis within the project could be strengthened by turning it into a mini-enterprise, in which children design, manufacture, market and sell T-shirts to raise money for a global charity.

Cross-curricular themes for informed citizens

The National Curriculum in England (DfEE/QCA 1999a) suggests that all subject areas, including design and technology, can promote learning across the curriculum in a number of areas such as spiritual, moral, social and cultural development. While we have dealt with cultural development comprehensively in Section Two, there are strong links between culture and citizenship (as emphasised in Chapters 2.1 and 3.1), and the other themes could be argued to provide essential experience and understanding for children in their growth as citizens. We will explore what awareness of each of these aspects can mean in the classroom, illustrating each with examples from design and technology projects.

Spiritual awareness

Spiritual education is often perceived as being strongly linked with religious education (as in the specific Christian meaning of the term in relation to the Holy Spirit). However, within the primary curriculum as currently defined, it is generally seen in a much wider context, as OFSTED and others have been at pains to point out: '"Spiritual" is not synonymous with "religious"; all areas of the curriculum may contribute to pupils' spiritual development' (OFSTED 1993).

Broadbent (1995: 6) sees *spirit* as a 'metaphor for that which animates us, which includes intellect, emotions, personality and personal commitments'. Such a definition is clearly founded on the notion of a 'self', and links with the development in children of self-awareness through their interactions with others. The products that children own or create in design and technology are part of the way they express (and maybe construct) this sense of self. Children can be asked: 'What does this toy/item of clothing etc. say about you?' Such a discussion can also introduce the idea of *materialism* – why do we define ourselves by the things we own? Does having too many *things* blind us to deeper realities? For example, the story Richard White told his class about the man who had given him a musical instrument in India (Chapter 2.4) tells us about what it means to be materially poor, but spiritually rich.

We should not forget, however, that an important aspect of spiritual development is *corporate*; for example, we often refer to a spirit of cooperation within a group. This can be fostered through collaboration between children in practically every aspect of a design and technology project, as we have emphasised throughout this book. For example, Case Study 13 (Chapter 3.4) explicitly addresses children's understanding of cooperation with a partner. It is this dimension of spiritual awareness – the shift from 'I' to 'we' – that can contribute most to children's understanding of what it means to be a citizen, by helping them to see themselves as part of, and having a responsibility for, wider groups within society, such as family, friends, school, community, and ultimately humankind.

Curricular definitions tend to associate spiritual education with a sense of awe, wonder and mystery in response to the natural world, itself the product of divine (or genetic) *creativity*. This is less often applied to the 'made' world created by humans, although such sensations are readily experienced when, for example, entering a cathedral. The construction of cathedrals over several centuries by medieval stonemasons and craftspeople illustrates what Ritchie (2001) has referred to as the interaction of 'head, hands and heart' in design and technology. Obviously it is the heart that most strongly corresponds to the spiritual for the purpose of this argument, encapsulating the personal motivation, faith and response to beauty of the designer-maker. Thus creativity and aesthetics, both strongly represented in design and technology, may be said to be explicitly spiritual in nature, as suggested by the National Curriculum order for the subject (DfEE/QCA 1999a: 8):

> Design and technology provides opportunities to promote spiritual development, through helping pupils recognise their own creativity and the creativity of others in finding solutions to problems, and through recognising the tension between material and non-material needs.

We need to ensure that children have opportunities to explore and evaluate special objects and environments (including, though not exclusively, those created as expressions of faith) exhibiting aesthetic beauty and evidence of creativity, such as musical instruments for QCA/DfEE Unit 5B: 'There is a sense of wonder at pupils' own achievements and in studying the work of talented designers and makers' (Coates and Rose 1999: 161).

Achievement in creating something of beauty as a response to such activities can reinforce children's sense of self-worth, yet failure can produce the opposite effect. We need to ensure, through the provision of appropriate FPTs, that children have sufficient support and scaffolding through a DMA to arrive at a satisfying outcome. For example, in helping Year 2 children produce Christmas cards with a sliding, lever, rotary or pop-up mechanism, teachers at Newbridge St. John's Infants' School in Bath provided examples of each mechanism and opportunities for children to try them out in paper before committing themselves to a choice for the DMA. Obviously, this project had a direct spiritual context in that it related to a Christian festival (although relatively few Christmas cards – and even fewer pop-ups – are explicitly religious in their symbolism). More significantly, it also contributed, along with many other design and technology experiences, to children's self-knowledge and personal growth through the application of qualities such as perseverance in the face of technical difficulties.

Moral awareness

Citizenship education is essentially moral education in that it is based on a communal ethic and norms of socially acceptable behaviour. However, what is socially acceptable tends to shift with time and between groups in society, with the result that we live in an era of moral relativism influenced by the postmodernist idea that there are no ultimate rights and wrongs. This climate invokes different responses; for politicians it can indicate a sense of moral decline within society, requiring didactic teaching of an imposed view of right and wrong in the classroom. The church and other religious leaders may call for a reintegration of the spiritual and moral dimensions of the curriculum, since one without the other is in their view dangerous. Many teachers tend to duck the issue of moral education through fear of indoctrination (Wilson 1990), yet their own moral standpoints (often morals in action rather than espoused morality) speak through their practice. What is clear is that, since education is an essentially human undertaking, some form of moral dimension is inescapable – as in the case of design and technology (see the discussion of values in Chapter 2.1).

In the context of citizenship education, we need to help children explore the tension between *individualism* (what is right for me) and *communalism* (what is right for the group, community etc.). This needs to match their cognitive and emotional development – for example, young children have a very clear sense of fair and unfair in relation to themselves: evidence of egocentrism in Piaget's view (1932). This can be extended to a wider appreciation of justice and injustice through the use of stories, as in the case study below (10). Another dimension of progression in this area is for children to move from externally imposed sets of rules motivated by fear of sanctions, to a higher state of working out moral principles for themselves (Piaget 1932). This can lead them ultimately to distinguish between what is lawful and what is moral, through discussion of well-chosen examples by the teacher, such as that of Swampy, the roads protestor. Children then need to be involved, both in the construction of rules and in confronting moral ambiguity and ethical dilemmas, for which stories (especially traditional tales) are an excellent vehicle:

> What is important ... is for rules to exist alongside educational measures which attempt to develop children's powers of practical moral wisdom. Stories are ideally suited for this latter purpose; to see them as a way of enforcing rules is to misunderstand their true moral potential.
>
> (Winston 1998: 130)

Case Study 10 – Citizenship through puppets (Year 1/2)

Introduction
This case study shows how retelling a traditional tale using puppets children have designed and made can raise moral issues and help children begin to understand how the rights and duties of a citizen (Jack – he of beanstalk fame) can sometimes conflict.

Setting the scene
Moira Hill, design and technology subject leader at Elm Park Primary School, Winterbourne, wanted to build on the sewing skills her Year 1/2 class had acquired during the previous term by undertaking a textiles-based project. She chose the QCA design and technology Unit 2B 'Puppets' from the whole-school plan since it also linked well with the literacy focus on traditional tales for that half term.

The teaching sequence
The children examined a selection of hand puppets and finger puppets made from a variety of materials. Each child was asked to find an example of a puppet to bring to the group and talk about. The children then practised basic sewing techniques and learned about making a paper

pattern in preparation for transfer to felt. The brief for the DMA asked groups to design and make puppets to retell a familiar traditional story (with good and bad characters).

Classroom organisation and differentiation
Moira decided to organise the class in small groups for the planning and making phase of the project, since the characters for each story would need to be developed together. With a mixed-age class she anticipated that some younger children would need additional support with stitching, so mixed the groups for fine motor control and had them working one at a time with an adult helper while the rest of the class were developing their scripts.

Planning the retelling of the tales was partly undertaken during Literacy Hour, which gave the children opportunities to discuss the characters and decide how they would add features to their puppets for recognition. For example, the wolf from *Little Red Riding Hood* was represented as fierce and malevolent (Fig. 3.2.1), whereas puppets representing children were given smiles. Moira decided to add features using a low-temperature glue gun or PVA glue. This method of appliqué enabled children to create some effective characterisations. The children negotiated their roles in the performance and selected a narrator. They had an opportunity to practise retelling the story of *Goldilocks and the Three Bears* during a Literacy Hour using a Barbie doll and three teddies!

Figure 3.2.1 The wolf puppet

Exploring moral issues through retelling Jack and the Beanstalk
The children evaluated their puppets through using them in performance. This enabled Moira to explore some of the moral dimensions of the stories; for example, is Jack a good or bad character? One child answered that he was both good and bad, because he stole the giant's eggs and chicken, but he also found the beans for his mum. Others thought that he was the hero of the story, and that it was OK to steal from giants because they eat people. The

only negative aspect of this action was that Jack 'might get caught'. Similar justifications were offered for the actions of other characters from traditional tales; Goldilocks was seen as a good character because 'she didn't know it was someone else's house, and she was starving'.

Discussion

The responses from these children indicate a relatively early stage in their moral development, focusing upon rules and sanctions rather than deeper issues of right and wrong. Winston (1998) reports on a drama project with a class of Year 2 children in which he took on various roles within the story of *Jack and the Beanstalk* and explored the tension between children's group moralities, i.e. loyalty to one's friends, courage displayed through risk-taking, and authoritarian moral codes prohibiting stealing, lying and disobedience. Children were able to recognise that Jack was a good friend but a naughty boy. It could be argued that such moral ambiguity was unhelpful for young children, yet the dilemmas faced by story characters can help children recognise at a basic level some of the tensions that a citizen might experience in deciding whether to follow a moral or lawful path in society. Such moral dilemmas face designers and technologists in developing new products, as acknowledged by the National Curriculum summary of the contribution of design and technology to moral development (DfEE/QCA 1999a). One moral criterion we might apply to a product is whether it denies individuals or groups their human rights, an important dimension of moral awareness that is clearly required for informed citizenship.

Human rights

The idea of human rights education is not new (Starkey 1991) but, like some of the other terms discussed in this chapter, it is enjoying a resurgence of interest at present as indicated by its inclusion within the National Scheme of Work for Citizenship at Key Stages 1 and 2 (QCA/DfEE 2001). In design and technology education, an appreciation of what we might mean by a right is raised by considering the difference between needs and wants when children come to identifying opportunities for their designs (Budgett-Meakin 1992). Another aspect that will be of particular relevance to the primary classroom is the increasing emphasis placed upon the rights of children – in what ways are these different from the rights of adults?

Children in Key Stage 2 might like to discuss the following list, compiled by Starkey (1991: 24) as a summary of the contents of various declarations of human rights. Which rights apply to children, and which to adults only?

Rights protected under these Conventions include the right to:

- life, survival and development;
- a name, a nationality and an identity to be preserved;
- liberty and security of person;
- not to be a slave;
- not to be tortured;
- the protection of the law;
- a fair and public hearing in the courts;
- privacy in home and correspondence;
- an adequate standard of living;
- education;
- leisure, play and artistic and cultural activities;
- marry and found a family;
- own property;

and these *fundamental freedoms*:

- freedom of thought, conscience and religion;
- freedom of opinion and expression;
- freedom of peaceful assembly and to join a trade union;
- freedom from unlawful attacks on honour and reputation;
- freedom of movement and residence.

It would also be interesting to consider which of the above rely on some form of technology for their fulfilment; for example it would be difficult to envisage providing an adequate standard of living without a supply of clean water, tools to till the soil, a form of shelter and clothing. An alternative context for such a project – if dealt with sensitively at Key Stage 2 – would be in considering the needs and rights of refugees and asylum-seekers. This topic features in the human rights unit within the Citizenship National Scheme of Work (QCA/DfEE 2001) and can raise the question of who is, and is not, a citizen. Why is citizenship so important to those who do not possess it?

In discussing the rights of children, Franklin (1986) draws distinctions between legal and moral rights, and also the potential conflict between rights to autonomy and protection. Protecting children from 'inadequate care, neglect and physical or emotional abuse in the home, or any other form of danger' (Franklin 1986: 14) will inevitably restrict their freedom. In relation to citizenship education, the key right that children do not possess is that to choose their government; they cannot vote, so in this important respect *children are not citizens*. They are disenfranchised from taking a full role in society, and as such can only play at citizenship in schools. These issues can be discussed in the classroom; for example, Year 5 children at Backwell Primary School, Weston-Super-Mare considered the rights children should have at different ages as part of their PSHE circle time.

Democracy

The notion of a citizen depends on the political system in which you live; it is a term most often used within liberal democracies, but would look very different in a totalitarian regime, or one based upon religious orthodoxy (e.g. the Taliban in Afghanistan). In the West, we tend to assume that democracy is a good thing, that it is somehow morally superior to other political systems or structures for organising society. For many minorities, however, democracy is the tyranny of the majority in which they cannot make their voices heard. This is a criticism that can be made particularly strongly of the first-past-the-post electoral system, in which the winner takes all and proceeds to dominate political life for a parliamentary term. Of course, politicians tell us that they listen to a wide range of opinions, but the extent to which they appear to respond more to the strong (media, business, military) than the weak can breed cynicism and alienation, particularly among the young:

> the experience of young people who do actively participate, albeit unconventionally through road protest for example, is that the structures and processes themselves frustrate genuine participation and a sense of being listened to. This points to the need to recognise informal networks and pressure groups as legitimate aspects of the democratic process and citizenship.
>
> (Maiteney and Wade 1999: 41)

Politics is another of those areas that primary teachers tend to avoid in the classroom, fearing the sudden appearance of angry parents anxious to protect the innocence of their children. Yet research evidence would suggest that 'people learn political identifications, knowledge, awareness of political problems, the capacity to discuss them, assess them and make decisions about them, at a much earlier stage than popular opinion imagines' (Franklin 1986: 42). Some schools hold mock elections at the same time as general elections, helping children to understand how the House of Commons is made up. A project to design the *system* by which votes could be canvassed, cast, collected and counted across the school would be a possible DMA.

However, few schools can be said to be genuinely democratic institutions. Teachers have so little control over their own professional lives that it is hardly surprising that they find the idea of giving children more say threatening. As children mature they will come to understand that what looks like democracy may actually be an instrument of social control. This too is an important lesson to learn about citizenship.

Social awareness

Liberal democracy is founded on the principle of social interchange within society. This can operate at many different levels, from personal relationships within the family to the power and economic relations that define our relative status, giving rise to labels such as socially disadvantaged. Undoubtedly, humans are social animals, yet our social instinct strives with the instinct for self-preservation, or tribal allegiance (to family, nation etc.). Genetic psychologists have coined the term 'selfish gene' to account for behaviours that place ourselves and our descendants before others. We live in an intensely individualistic society, partly as a result of defining ourselves materially – in terms of the things we own rather than the people we love. Designers must share some of the blame for this as a result of their success in creating seductive products, in particular those that isolate us from human contact, such as electronic games. This can be used as an evaluation criterion during an IEA: is this product designed to be shared by people? Will it help people to become friends or make them spend more time on their own? Another social aspect of such evaluation could relate to status symbols or peer pressure when choosing what to buy: 'The critical evaluation of existing products might involve pupils asking whether we buy products that reflect our status in society and social values' (Coates and Rose 1999: 164).

If children bring in their own belongings (toys, trainers, clothes) to evaluate, we are much more likely to get at the real reasons for their decisions, helping them to understand the social context of technology.

At the level of individual relationships, we have all seen how difficult it is for young children to work and play cooperatively. We say that they need 'socialising' into the school setting, but to an extent perhaps this inevitably implies crushing their individuality. It is a fine line to tread between individual creativity and collaborative working, but all children need to develop an awareness of the needs of others in order to succeed in design and technology. As suggested in the National Curriculum (DfEE/QCA 1999a: 8), this is the main way in which the subject can contribute to social development 'through helping pupils recognise the need to consider the view of others when discussing design ideas'.

Fundamentally, design and technology requires what Goleman (1994) describes as 'emotional intelligence'. He defines this as an amalgam of abilities, 'such as being able to motivate oneself and persist in the face of frustrations; to control impulse and delay gratification; to regulate one's moods and keep distress from swamping the ability to think; to empathise and to hope' (1994: 34). Such attributes (which, claims Goleman, can be taught and learned) are far more telling predictors of success in our careers and relationships than exam results or IQ scores. Being emotionally intelligent allows us to understand ourselves and empathise with others, faculties which Howard Gardner (1983) termed *intrapersonal* and *interpersonal* respectively, within his theory of 'multiple intelligences'. It is this social domain that also underpins success in the adult world of work – another defining feature of citizenship that children do not yet share.

Work-related learning

One of the primary motivations behind the introduction of technological subjects in the secondary curriculum was *vocational* (Layton 1995), to prepare less academic pupils for industry. Although the model we now have in primary schools is much more educationally oriented, design and technology is still seen as one of the main routes through which children come to an understanding of capitalist economics, as illustrated by the following statement from the National Curriculum (DfEE/QCA 1999a: 9):

> through bringing a realistic industrial or commercial perspective to the development of a product in the classroom, visiting a workplace for hands-on experience related to designing and making, and providing the opportunity for visitors from business to act as product advisers or clients.

There is relatively little evidence of this kind of practice in most primary schools. The QCA National Scheme of Work does not require children to take their ideas beyond prototypes. There are some mini-enterprise projects at primary level in which pupils undertake the design, production and marketing of items such as hand-made stationery (Watts 1991) or screen-printed T-shirts (see above), yet these activities are the exception rather than the rule. There are, however, examples of children working with professional designers (see Chapter 1.4) sometimes on projects that will be taken into production. The opera project (Case Study 7, Chapter 2.3) involved children gaining an understanding of how a theatre set and costume designer works to a brief set by the director. Young children at Chater Infants' School, Watford designed classroom furniture after interviewing a designer about his role in the company (Chapter 3.4). A further example is of a class of Year 6 pupils at Western Road Primary School, Lewes, who were commissioned by Drusilla's Zoo Park in Sussex to design a new enclosure for their meerkats (Davies 1991). The children spent time observing the creatures' behaviour and worked closely with the zoo's designer to create an environment that simulated the meerkats' South African homeland, while allowing maximum access for viewing them at close range. Seeing their ideas actually constructed on a large scale with resistant materials helped them appreciate some of the constraints within which professional designers have to work.

The official documents on economic and industrial understanding across the curriculum (e.g. NCC 1990c) rarely discuss whether the purpose of such education is to promote the enterprise culture or to develop a critique of the political economy (Ross 1992). In fact it is the former that is usually envisaged, preparing children for 'future economic roles: as producers, consumers and citizens in a democracy' (NCC 1990c: 1). The technology curricula of some countries make this even more explicit; for example that for Western Australia is entitled 'Technology and Enterprise'. Yet, as part of their education for social awareness, children can be allowed to question the inequalities within our economy:

> Young children, with their sense of fairness, will with minimal encouragement raise questions such as:
>
> - salary differentials;
> - gender roles in the workplace;
> - ethnic roles in the workplace;

- the notion of 'fair profit' (as opposed to what the market will bear)

- conditions of employment; and

- staff/worker differentials.

(Ross 1992: 59)

Such questioning – if undertaken sensitively – could add an extra critical dimension to the standard visit to a local supermarket as part of a food technology project.

Indeed, research into children's ideas about economics (Linton 1990) suggests that they find the notions of profit and interest morally indefensible. Children at age eight have developed some of the underlying economic concepts such as reciprocity, equivalence and conservation, but they tend to view the market from the consumer's viewpoint (naturally!). Role-play activities in the classroom in which children set up shops or other businesses (such as the estate agency in Chapter 3.4) can help to broaden their perspective, while creating opportunities for designing and making products for sale and promotion materials.

Summary

This chapter has dealt with the contribution that awareness of a wide range of issues can make to children's understanding of their developing roles as citizens. We have chosen to relate this awareness to technological literacy – an appreciation of the messages which technological products convey, their cultural dependency and inherent issues of power. Because technology is such a potent symbol within the society we inhabit, it is vital that children begin to interpret and question it in order to take a full part within that society. The phase of a primary design and technology project that best lends itself to dealing explicitly with issues of spiritual, moral, human rights, democratic, social and economic awareness is the IEA. Accordingly most of the examples given have involved the evaluation of products, although the main case study has shown how moral issues can be raised with children through the retelling of traditional tales using puppets.

Developing skills for citizenship through design and technology

Purpose of this chapter

Through reading this chapter you will gain:

- an appreciation of the potential for design and technology activity to develop a range of skills that will underpin children's future citizenship

- an understanding of how these skills draw upon the *awareness* explored in Chapter 3.2 and prepare children for the *action* of Chapter 3.4

- an ability to critique the notion of key transferable skills in the primary curriculum.

Introduction

The current National Curriculum is concerned, to a greater extent than its predecessors, with the development of cross-curricular, transferable skills in children. For example, it lists *thinking skills* to be addressed across the curriculum, which are described as enabling children to 'learn how to learn':

- Information-processing skills

- Reasoning skills

- Enquiry skills

- Creative thinking skills

- Evaluation skills

This list reads almost like an outline of processes children go through during a DMA: researching the brief; evaluating existing products and their own work; generating creative ideas etc. In design and technology literature these are usually referred to as process skills, implying that this term can be applied to activities that are more complex and abstract than, say, using a particular tool correctly. Thinking skills in the National Curriculum, as well as closely mirroring those involved in designing and making, are also prerequisites for citizenship. For example, the ability to process information from official sources (the media, the government etc.), evaluate it and come to an opinion is a useful set of skills for anyone intending to vote, lobby or take action on a particular issue. We shall exemplify each briefly below.

Thinking skills in design and technology

Information-processing skills

In researching their topic on musical instruments, the Year 4 classes at Bromley Heath Junior School, South Gloucestershire (Chapter 2.4) gathered information from a number of sources: the Internet, CD-ROMs, books, parents etc. They needed to sift and summarise this information in order to present it to the rest of the class, and extract that which was of most use in designing their own instruments.

Reasoning skills

The environmental projects discussed in Chapter 3.4, in which children had to justify their decisions about what kind of action to take in response to a problem, exemplify reasoning skills in action. When deciding whether to develop a machine for removing graffiti, or a community whiteboard where young people could exercise their artistic skills, the children at St. James' CE Primary School in Bermondsey had to weigh up evidence and present a proposal to the rest of the class. Reasoning skills can also come into play when we are figuring out how something works; for example the children looking at torches in Durand Primary School, South London (Case Study 4, Chapter 2.2) had to think through the internal mechanical and electrical connections that made up the circuit. McCormick (1999) calls the outcome of this kind of reasoning 'device knowledge', which is a specifically *technological* understanding of how things work and fit together.

Enquiry skills

Enquiry is often perceived as a scientific process (see 'Scientific Enquiry Sc1' DfEE/QCA 1999c) so if we want to develop children's enquiry skills through design and technology, projects with a science link would appear to offer most potential. For example, when the children at Ridge Junior School were designing security lighting (Case Study 11 below) they had to ask the question 'How can we alert the people inside the house that someone is entering the gate?' They researched relevant electric circuits and predicted the effects of the switches they were designing, testing the outcomes to evaluate their effectiveness.

Creative thinking and evaluation skills

These areas are both covered in some depth within the first section of this book (Chapters 1.3 and 1.4), including a discussion of how we might go about teaching such skills to children explicitly.

Key skills in the National Curriculum

The same links with design and technology can be made for another list of cross-curricular skills in curriculum documentation, the so-called key skills, to which we have added specific design and technology examples:

- *Communication*, through presenting design ideas in drawings, models and verbally.

- *Application of number*, through the use of accurate measurement in drawing and making.

- *Information technology*, through the use of the Internet and CD-ROMs for researching a design brief, drawing software for communicating ideas, spreadsheets for costing materials, digital cameras for recording process and marketing outcomes.

- *Working with others*, through the operation of multidisciplinary design teams.

- *Improving own learning and performance*, through structured reflection and evaluation at various stages of a DMA.

- *Problem-solving*, through creative approaches to open and closed practical situations.

Of the two lists of skills outlined above, this set of key skills is the one upon which most emphasis has been placed to date – at least in secondary and further education – and which will therefore have the greatest impact upon the work of primary teachers in the near future. The use of the analogies 'key' and 'core' begs a series of questions. Which 'lock' are these skills the 'key' to? Are they to be seen as the 'core' of the curriculum 'apple' (which is usually the bit thrown away when the rest has been eaten)? According to Tribe (1996: 22) there are two assumptions that lie at the heart of the whole notion: 'that skills should be generic and that skills should be transferable. The term "generic" implies that the skill is found and used in a wide variety of occupations whilst the term transferable implies that skills that are learnt in one context can be applied to others'.

Unfortunately, there is little research evidence to suggest that such skills are either generic or transferable (Green 1997). Hyland and Johnson (1998: 163) go so far as to suggest that such 'free-standing, context-independent abilities … are without philosophical and empirical support and are entirely illusory'. It is certainly difficult to find a clearly articulated rationale for the key skills agenda. Rather than going back to first principles, each successive government initiative in this area has tended to rely on the previous one for its underpinning. In many classrooms, children exhibit the symptoms of 'situated cognition' (McCormick *et al.* 1995) – what they learn in one context they can only apply (if at all) in the same context. The existence of generic skills is unproven: 'There is a jump from performing an action or task skilfully to the identification of a discrete or substantive *skill* possessed by the performer' (Hyland and Johnson 1998: 169).

Does such a criticism undermine what we are trying to demonstrate in this book – that children's work in design and technology can develop in them the attributes of creativity, sensitivity to culture and skills for citizenship? It certainly prompts us to tread carefully. The qualities and learning outcomes that children in our case studies exhibit may not be evident in another context. But this does not invalidate them; they are examples of what children are capable of in the right situation. Furthermore, the transfer process may be somewhat more complex than we have imagined. For example, if a child has the perception that 'I can use ICT', developed through a design and technology activity, it may be the *attitude* or *confidence* that is transferred to other learning situations, rather than the skill itself. They may be using a very *different* set of ICT skills in writing a letter to their MP from those involved in producing a spreadsheet to cost their design and technology project, but successful experience in one context will breed confidence in the other. Alternatively, a key skill such as communication may be exercised within a DMA (e.g. by children presenting their ideas to the rest of the class) before being used during a debate in citizenship education. In this case, design and technology may *enhance* an existing set of skills. The following project illustrates a number of the key skills in action.

Case Study 11 – Lighting it up (Year 4)

Introduction
This case study shows how a design and technology unit of work can begin to address issues surrounding security and surveillance in society, through a project concerned with electrical control. The children used their ICT skills to design a system for triggering a light when visitors passed through a gate.

Setting the scene
This unit was planned as part of a Lifelong Learning Project, in which ICT-literate pupils from local secondary schools worked with pupils at Ridge Junior School in Yate, South Gloucestershire. The initiative was supported by Learning Partnerships West and South Gloucestershire Council, releasing Martin Palmer, the deputy head teacher and design and technology subject leader. Although the principal focus was upon control technology, Martin was keen to involve elements of PSHE/citizenship as this is central to the ethos of lifelong learning. Effective communication and sensitivity between primary and secondary pupils was essential to the success of the partnership, and Martin was also keen that children should appreciate some of the social impact of technology – particularly the widespread use of security lights, cameras and alarms. He wanted to reinforce the learning about electrical circuits that his Year 4 class had studied during the previous year.

Teaching sequence
Martin followed the QCA Unit 4E 'Lighting it up', with some modifications. He used an hour per week, together with some science and ICT time. The topic started with an emphasis on the health and safety aspects of electricity, with the class drawing up a set of rules to keep safe. This required the ability to negotiate and arrive at a shared understanding of the dangers children face. Next the children investigated light sources. They used books, the Internet and CD-ROMs to draw together a collection of different kinds of lamp. Martin brought in several electrical components for handling and discussion and children answered a series of questions about how lights are used to keep us safe.

Later in the project the emphasis shifted towards circuits and their use in controlling lights. Through a hands-on formative assessment activity, Martin was pleased to find that all the children had remembered how to construct a simple circuit from their Year 3 science work. He then showed them how a switch could be used to activate a security light (for example attached to a garden gate). Groups of children designed and made prototype control circuits for LEGO model houses, incorporating different switch mechanisms. Some modelled circuits on a CD-ROM, changing bulbs and resistors while evaluating the outcomes. Children were asked to consider the effects of their designs upon those living in and visiting the houses. A and J (Fig. 3.3.1) used a swing barrier design to control access to their house, in which the security light would come on when the barrier was raised. It was important for these children to consider the negative aspects of security lights (increasing distrust and fear of crime, light pollution) as part of their evaluation.

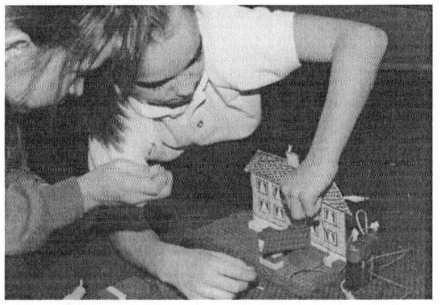

Figure 3.3.1 A and J use a swing barrier design to control security lighting on their house

Discussion – coverage of key skills

Communication was essential to this project, especially when children were explaining their projects to the visiting secondary pupils. They needed to *apply numeracy skills* in matching the ratings of lamps to those of the batteries in their alarm designs. *Information technology* was an important feature of the project throughout and the children learned that *working with others* (mainly in pairs) was essential to developing *problem-solving* strategies for getting the security light triggers to function effectively. It was necessary to evaluate these devices, not only to help children *improve their own learning and performance*, but to consider some of the wider social and citizenship issues raised by the project.

The notion of transferability within the key skills debate underlies the rationale for FPTs in design and technology. We teach children specific skills in short activities so that they will be equipped to use them as part of a DMA. In the following example, children were taught techniques for cutting and shaping fruit and vegetables safely and hygienically. They then transferred these skills to the task of designing an individual salad.

Case Study 12 – Eat more fruit and vegetables (Year 1)

Introduction
This case study shows how young children can decide upon their own rules for keeping healthy and safe when working with food in the classroom. In doing so they exhibited skills of communication, negotiating with the teacher and each other to arrive at a consensus. They went on to put these rules into practice, while developing manual skills to cut and shape fruit and vegetables as part of a salad.

Setting the scene
Julia Sutcliffe is the deputy head teacher and design and technology coordinator at Old Sodbury Primary School, South Gloucestershire. In the Autumn term, the Year 1 children (5–6 years old) in her infant class were following QCA design and technology Unit 1C 'Eat more fruit and vegetables'. She was particularly keen to emphasise the health and hygiene aspects of the fruit and vegetables topic. She felt that positive messages about a balanced diet with plenty of fruit and vegetables would have an effect upon children's eating habits in the school dining hall and at home. She also wanted them to get into the habits of washing their hands before eating and working hygienically with food in future design and technology projects.

Julia decided to link this unit with the school harvest festival, which gave her the opportunity of considering wider issues with the children, such as 'Where do our fruit and vegetables come from?' 'Do the people who grow them get a fair price?' 'Why are some people in the world hungry?' She also decided to bring in examples such as sweet potatoes to draw the

---

children's attention to the varied diets within our multicultural society. Old Sodbury is a small village in a predominantly white rural area and Julia felt it important that children should begin to recognise that they were part of a larger society that includes people with different tastes and cultural backgrounds (see Chapter 2.4).

The teaching sequence
Once children had observed the fruit and vegetables provided using a range of senses (sight, touch, smell, taste), Julia asked them to sort them into groups according to different criteria: by shape, hardness, whether they were eaten raw or cooked etc. Some children required extra support with this activity since they were unfamiliar with many of the fruit and vegetables in their unprocessed state. Julia was surprised that so many had difficulty in naming even quite common examples. The children next drew the inside and outside of fruit and vegetables cut in half, giving them an appreciation of structure and texture. They cut out photographs from fruit and vegetable information leaflets provided by the local supermarket, health centre and hospital, and assembled their own collage (a sort of 'virtual' salad). Julia felt that she should have collected these leaflets earlier in the year – the harvest festival had given many other schools similar ideas and stocks were low!

The next lesson started with a discussion about rules and their purposes, before the children made suggestions for their own set of rules for keeping safe with food. Initially, children's ideas were focused on the physical safety aspects; one child suggested 'don't throw fruit' as a rule, whereupon another chipped in with 'don't throw vegetables'. This is evidence of their limited experience of different types of rules: they modelled their suggestions very closely upon things that had been said to them in the classroom or playground. The idea of hygiene and 'keeping safe from germs' had to be introduced to them, but once they realised what was required, they agreed the following list:

- Don't throw fruit or vegetables
- Don't use a knife with a point
- Wash your hands with soap
- Wash the vegetables or fruit
- Clean the tables
- Clean the chopping boards
- Wear a cooking apron

Children then applied these rules when practising the skills to shape fruit and vegetables using different tools. As they worked, they described the effects of slicing, grating and squeezing, while being introduced to words such as 'squash', 'shred' and 'juice' (Fig. 3.3.2). Afterwards they recorded their activity in drawing, to help them remember the techniques for when they would need to use them in the DMA.

For the DMA, Julia asked the children to design their own vegetable salad. She had collected individual plastic salad containers from the local supermarket and encouraged children to think carefully about presentation. They had to provide her with a list of ingredients (no more than six for budgetary reasons) which she purchased for the following week. As part of the planning for making, they had to write instructions, showing someone else how to make it, including some of the shaping words introduced during the FPT. Because of space constraints

Figure 3.3.2 Developing fruit squeezing and juicing skills

in the classroom, children actually made their salads in small groups with a learning support assistant (LSA) in the school kitchen. During the making they discussed and observed the safety rules they had earlier drawn up, and took the final products home to eat. The following day they talked about what they had liked about the salad. The positive comments from this session, together with the written evaluative comments from the parents convinced Julia that she had succeeded in changing children's attitudes towards vegetables, as well as developing key citizenship-related skills such as cooperation, and attitudes such as respect for a diversity of tastes. With hindsight she would have asked the children to eat some of the salad at school so that she could have prompted more detailed evaluations for assessment purposes.

Discussion

The skills of working with fruit and vegetables might not seem at first sight to be relevant to citizenship. However, consider how much less confident these children would be as adults without the ability to prepare food or access the wide range of fruit and vegetables available to us in a multicultural society. The skills children learned through this project led to increased *confidence* in one area that could be transferred to other aspects of their lives. Furthermore, these skills were to work with food *safely and hygienically*; the ability to keep clean and healthy, together with understanding of conditions likely to lead to disease, are clear requirements for every citizen.

Summary

In this chapter we have considered some of the skills children need to develop in order to take on roles as citizens. We have reviewed the lists of thinking skills and key skills within the National Curriculum, looking at how they relate to each other and to the role of the FPT within a design and technology project. In particular, the chapter has questioned the extent to which these skills can really be regarded as transferable between different subjects or educational contexts. The role of design and technology – with its own set of high level process skills – is vital here in contributing to the development in children of the confidence to use a range of skills in different situations, as demonstrated by case studies drawn from Key Stages 1 and 2. We next need to look at how children might build upon this confidence and practise the skills of *active citizenship* through DMAs.

Creating sustainable futures through participation

Purpose of this chapter

Through reading this chapter you will gain:

- an appreciation of the scope and limitations of active citizenship in the primary curriculum

- an understanding of what *sustainable development* and *global citizenship* might look like in practice

- strategies for planning DMAs that make use of appropriate technology to address real or fantasy needs.

Introduction

In the introductory chapter of this book we suggested a couple of possible technological futures for the planet: a 'doomsday scenario' or a 'high-tech utopia'. While neither of these might seem particularly attractive propositions, they both point up humanity's need for a creative response. Whatever the thinking that has served us well in the past, it will be inadequate to meet the demands of the future. Since design and technology is a future-oriented activity, it has the potential to empower children to imagine a society and environment which is better than that which they currently inhabit. Creative teaching is called for, which helps children engage with global issues and provides them with the necessary skills to make positive changes in their environment.

In the original National Curriculum for Technology (DES/WO 1990), design and technology was supposed to take place within five specific contexts: home, school, community, recreation, business and industry. Each of these contexts (or cultures – see Chapter 2.1) is a potential setting for children's active participation in projects to improve some aspect of the lives of people near and far. Although the contexts for design and technology activity are no longer specified in the current National Curriculum, they live on in some of the units of work within the National Scheme (QCA/DfEE 1998). For example, Unit 1B 'Playgrounds' is set within a school or community context, whereas Unit 4E 'Lighting it up' could be set within a leisure or business and industry context. Central to the liberal-republican model of citizenship within the National Curriculum is the notion of the active citizen who becomes involved at a local, national and global level to improve situations that affect themselves and others. This chapter will show how, through DMAs, children can begin to take on this role.

Children's views of the future

The best place to start when considering how to plan classroom experiences that will allow children to respond creatively is with their own ideas. Hicks and Holden (1995) report on a survey of children's visions of the future. They found that while half the children at age seven thought about their own personal futures often, less than a quarter reflected on the future for their local area. Encouragingly, 41 per cent claimed to think about the future of the world often, with a further third considering it sometimes. While the majority considered that their own futures would improve, they were less optimistic about other people and the planet as a whole. Eleven-year-olds in particular were worried about increasing pollution, poverty and wars: 'Their choice for preferred futures indicates that many would like a future based on greater environmental awareness and their action as individuals reinforces this as an area of concern' (Hicks and Holden 1995: 78).

These findings will not surprise any teacher who has discussed global issues with his/her class. The problem lies (as with all of us) in the differences between what children say and what they do. At a mundane level, their apparently wasteful use of resources in a design and technology project (cutting a circle out of the middle of a piece of card for example) may frustrate us. Often it is because they have not made the connections between the big ideas of environmentalism (e.g. deforestation) and their individual choices (how much paper to use). Education for sustainable futures is about making those links and helping children to act on them.

Sustainable futures

Sustainable development is a theme that finds strong expression in the current National Curriculum, originally defined by the World Commission on Environment and Development (1987: 1) as: 'development that meets the needs of the present without compromising the ability of future generations to meet their own needs'. It needs to be distinguished from the concept of sustainable growth, which is an altogether less radical proposal working within the assumptions of capitalist economics: national economies must expand, production and consumption must increase. Sustainable development questions these assumptions, taking a much longer term view.

Education for sustainable development has its roots in the environmental education initiatives of the 1970s and 1980s. Children's voices in research findings indicate that they are already concerned about environmental destruction, growing crime and violence and social inequality both locally and globally (Hicks and Holden 1995). Furthermore they wish to be active in working towards effective change to ensure improved social and environmental conditions. The QCA working party addressing this theme has chosen to define it in the following terms:

> Education for sustainable development enables pupils to develop the knowledge, values and skills to participate in decisions about the way we do things individually and collectively, both locally and globally, that will improve the quality of life now without damaging the planet for the future.
>
> (Panel for Education for Sustainable Development 1998: 10)

They offer some concrete suggestions about how to implement this aspect of the curriculum in the classroom (QCA 1999). This lists the values and dispositions; skills and aptitudes; and knowledge and understanding that every child should have developed by the end of each Key Stage. These are grouped under seven broad headings:

- Interdependence
- Citizenship and stewardship
- Needs and rights of future generations
- Diversity
- Quality of life, equity and justice
- Sustainable change
- Uncertainty, and precaution in action

For example, the learning outcomes for the end of Key Stage 1 include the requirement for children to:

- understand the concept of finite resources
- have begun to understand the role of the individual and others in the

consumption of resources, and the need for the four 'R's – reduction of consumption, re-use, repair, recycle.

The progression within Key Stage 2 is quite steep, leading to some challenging outcomes, including that children should:

- have begun to understand the concepts of carrying capacity and limits through, for example, studying overgrazing or road capacity

- be able to understand how human systems work in terms of simple systems concepts as inputs, outputs, sources, sinks and flows, and

- consider how they may be managed more sustainably, for example the house, the school, and the farm.

If we look at the above list, it becomes immediately obvious that several points relate directly to our consumption and disposal of *designed* and *manufactured* products; design and technology clearly has a role to play here. Goggin and Lawler (1998) comment on the recent growth of awareness among designers of the sustainability of resources, manufacturing techniques and maintenance in the products they develop, leading to the notion of *eco-design*:

> Designers have begun to recognise that reducing the environmental impact of products requires a life-cycle approach. What this means is that at every stage in a product's life-cycle materials and energy are used and waste and pollution are created ... With an understanding of the many environmental impacts of a product during its life-cycle – from cradle to grave – it is possible to target design efforts to reduce impact.
> (Goggin and Lawler 1998: 108)

In the design and technology curriculum, this might be translated into strategies such as *eco-logging* in which children audit the use of materials and energy in a product they have been asked to evaluate. At a later stage they can be presented with *eco-choice* points in a project in which they are given the relevant environmental information to make sustainable decisions.

Rogers (1997) reports on an initiative with primary trainee teachers in which they were asked to reflect upon issues such as sustainability and eco-design, then asked to teach a short unit of design and technology in school relating to these themes. Being required to engage with the issues as part of classroom planning forced trainees to think about sustainability in greater depth. Using a framework of questions compiled by Buck and Inman (1992) to 'unpack' various global issues in the classroom, trainees found that children became completely involved. One trainee was teaching a mixed class of 7–9-year-olds. Combining the design and technology project with a history topic on the Romans, she took the idea of designing an interactive display, used in college, to help the children understand:

> the processes the Romans went through to grow their own grain, fruit and vegetables and raise and butcher animals for meat. After comparing and contrasting this with modern-day experiences, the children were able to recognise continuity in foods including fish, chicken, olive oil, honey, carrots, celery. The children gained an understanding of modern day dependence on less local supplies and the transporting and importing that takes place to provide us with the foods we need.
>
> (Rogers 1997: 117)

Clearly, this approach required children to develop an understanding of another time and culture (Chapter 2.4), but it was also used to introduce the notion of global citizenship described in Chapter 3.1. Children were able to relate the transport issues in another historical and geographical context to those in our own society, where huge lorries ferry food around our roads to supply supermarkets, which many of us in turn drive to. The ability to relate big problems to a local context is the key to involving children in sustainable design and technology projects that can really benefit the environment, rather than leaving children feeling powerless in the face of the challenges facing the world.

Appropriate technology

Appropriate contexts for eco-design projects include transport (as above), clothing, energy-efficient homes and packaging (QCA/DfEE 1998 Unit 3A). For example, McGarry (1992) offers the following set of questions to be used when investigating packaging:

- What is appropriate packaging?
- What is it for?
- Does it need to be waterproof or airtight?
- Does it need to be protected from knocks?
- How many layers does it need?
- Will it be bio-degradable or recyclable?
- How much has existing packaging to do with advertising?
- Is the item to be packaged worth producing?

This notion of appropriateness in technology was originally developed by E. F. Schumacher in *Small is Beautiful* (1973). It led to the formation of the Intermediate Technology (IT) charity, which works with communities in the Majority World to develop technology produced using simple means, with local materials, local labour and low-cost capital equipment. The values such products should exhibit include a concern for smallness, simplicity, capital cheapness and non-violence. The message of sustainable development education is that such technology is appropriate not only for the economically less developed majority, but for the economically more developed minority – the affluent north – as well. It is also singularly appropriate for primary classrooms, where the simplicity and low-cost requirements are of particular importance.

Active citizenship – degrees of participation

We want children to become active in developing creative and appropriate solutions to environmental and social problems. But how involved do we want them to get? Hart (cited in Buck and Inman 1992) has proposed a model for progression in participation, characterising the levels at which adults allow children to get involved:

1   Manipulation (*e.g. pre-school children carry political placards*)

2   Decoration (*children provide useful images for a campaign*)

3   Tokenism (*children sit on a panel, but without briefing*)

4   Assigned but informed (*know about the issue, told what to do*)

5   Consulted and informed (*know about, and asked about, the issue*)

6   Adult-initiated shared decisions with children

7   Child-initiated shared decisions with adults

8   Child-initiated and directed

According to Hart, the first three 'steps' of this ladder do not really involve children's participation at all. The others imply increasing levels of participation, but are not really hierarchical in that it is possible to plan a project at any level depending on circumstance. For example, the idea for a project to construct a school pond could come from the staff, with the children helping to dig it (level 4). Alternatively they could be asked about where it should be, what shape etc. (level 5) or involved in designing it (level 6). Alternatively, children may have proposed the idea and are given the opportunity to carry it through (level 7) or even to direct adults in digging it (level 8)!

A limited response?

One criticism of the model of citizenship education proposed in the Crick Report (QCA 1998) is that it allows children to consider big issues but then severely constrains the responses they can make (Gibson and Backus 2001). For example, the draft unit of work on children's/human rights for the National Scheme of Work for Citizenship (QCA/DfEE 2001: 2) suggests that children: 'Working with partners or in groups create a "Charter of Rights" for home, class, school … society as a whole'. The suggested action children can take on human rights, however, is to consider what can be done to improve the running of the classroom.

This is certainly an example of 'thinking globally and acting locally' (Agenda 21 from the Rio Earth Summit of 1990) but is it an adequate response to the issue? If we are to talk about empowering children it must surely go beyond allocating monitors for the classroom. The old adage that we should have the 'courage to change the things we can, the humility to accept those we can't change, and the wisdom to know the difference' is surely relevant here. There may be structural problems in society or the world at large that children will want to challenge forcefully – even by taking unlawful action in extreme cases – but the classroom is not the place for it. What is possible within the 'establishment' institution of school is a rather more restricted response; although we must try to make the activities as real as possible for children.

An example of a school in which the staff wanted to involve children in real decisions is Chater Infants' School in Watford. The provision of a new school building was used as an opportunity to involve children in the consultation and design process (Davies 1992). Children drew up lists of their requirements for an ideal school building and sent plans to the architects, who took into account their users' requirements in the final design. When it came to fitting storage furniture, the designer from Papworth Group came and talked to the children in Key Stage 1 about how he went about the process of designing and making – asking lots of questions to find out exactly what would need to be stored and how it would be accessed. The children made use of this approach when looking at areas of the classroom where there was a need for specialist storage: the book corner and the music area. By going on to prototype storage units and a keyboard stand they had a clear sense that they were involved in making important changes to their classroom environment.

Planning an active citizenship project

The starting point for all such initiatives should always be a thorough exploration of the issue(s) to be addressed. This should certainly involve as many colleagues as possible, but a classroom discussion at an early stage will also increase children's sense of ownership and the potential level of their participation (see above). Hicks (1995) has offered a framework of questions to facilitate this process:

1 What is the issue?

What do we think, feel, hope and fear in relation to this particular issue? What do others who are involved think, feel and say?

2 How has it come about?

Why do we and others think, feel and act the way we do? What and who has influenced us and others involved? What is the history of this situation?

3 Who gains, who loses?

Who has the power in this situation and how do they use it? Is it used to the advantage of some and the disadvantage of others?

4 What is our vision?

What would things look like in a more just, peaceful and sustainable future, for ourselves and for others? What values will we see to guide our choices?

5 What can be done?

What are the possible courses of action open to us? What are others already doing? Which course of action is most likely to achieve our vision of a preferred future?

Taking the outcomes of this process (recorded on flip chart or sugar paper – recycled!) you can then begin to put together a unit of work that describes what children will actually be doing on a week-by-week basis. If your project involves improving the school playground, the Learning Through Landscapes Trust provides a range of support, ideas and expertise that will help in this process. The first few sessions will inevitably involve research: contacting the local council if applicable to find out what plans exist; searching local newspapers, political newsletters, Internet sites so that children are as well informed as possible. Contacting potential sources of help – parents, local building firms, suppliers etc. – could also form part of this initial phase. Next children need to have the opportunity to put forward design proposals, either working individually or in pairs. These can be in text form (produced during extended writing in literacy), sketches, simple card or paper models. There should be a session set aside for them to present their ideas to the whole class for scrutiny and questions, followed by a vote on the preferred option to take forward. It may be necessary to develop the ideas further at this stage; some aspects can perhaps be contracted out to other groups within the class.

Depending on the project, the final presentation may be to governors or others involved in implementing the work. The unit of work could stop here, because any subsequent action the children take may be out of school, or at least removed from the formal curriculum. Alternatively, you may feel that this real making phase is an important part of the design and technology project which needs to be planned for, although it may not involve more than a small group of children at any one time, working with a knowledgeable adult outside the classroom. The following projects exemplify this planning approach in practice.

At Our Lady of Lourdes RC Primary School in Kingswood, just outside Bristol, the environmental awareness of pupils has been raised dramatically by a class project on recycling. The school has an environmental strategy, part of which involves two environmentally aware people (EAPs) being identified from each class to play a leading role in activities such as litter collection and recycling projects. Litter had been an ongoing concern in the school and in the recent past older children had been trying to design lids for the playground bins which would prevent litter blowing out. Jayne McCarthy, who has a Year 3/4 class, actually planned the work through a QCA geography scheme of work unit ('Improving the environment'), but the opportunities for design and technology were clear. The class, with support from an education officer from the Recycling Consortium (a local environment organisation), conducted a litter audit (over three days) for the whole school (except the kitchens) and analysed the results. Unsurprisingly, paper was the most common type of waste collected. The discussion of the categories of litter helped increase the pupils' awareness of what is thrown away and how this could be reduced. At a small-scale, but very practical level, they were taught how to fold crisp packets to make them less likely to be blown out of bins and around the playground.

Jayne then taught about the long-term effects on global warming of their attitudes towards energy and rubbish, and introduced children to the benefits of recycling. This led to them emailing the Recycling Consortium to ask for appropriate recycling boxes for the school. There was discussion about where the boxes should be placed to maximise the benefits – the decision to place one next to the photocopier in the library was uncontroversial! They then planned and ran an assembly for the whole school aimed at increasing other pupils' awareness of the issues and commitment to using the recycling boxes. The crisp packet technique has almost become a playground craze, with pupils from Jayne's class regularly being asked for demonstrations of how to fold the 'crisp triangles'. A few weeks later, Jayne asked the children to evaluate the impact of the recycling boxes with some practical maths involved in estimating and measuring the amount collected in different locations.

Although planned by the teacher to address learning objectives in geography, the project involved the children in identifying needs, planning to meet those needs and implementing their plans – processes clearly closely related to design and technology. Other design and technology work could easily be linked to such a project. For example, the children could have designed and made their own recycling containers or desktop litter collectors (see Ritchie 2001). Posters and other methods of encouraging recycling could have been produced targeted at particular age groups. Alternative ways of packaging lunches brought to school could have been considered in order to reduce waste materials. An alternative approach is illustrated by Whitehall Primary School in Bristol, where pupils used materials collected in recycling bins in their school to make entries for a local 'Rubbish Revolution DIY Furniture' competition. This had the added economic advantage of saving on consumable resources.

Another example of a design and technology project designed to address a local environmental problem was that undertaken by a Year 6 class at St. James' CE Primary School in Bermondsey. Children had noticed that the subway running underneath the nearby main road was covered in graffiti. They developed a range of ideas for deterring graffiti artists, including changing the surface of the tunnel walls and designing a machine which would squirt detergent and wipe the walls as it passed through the subway (this was tested using a range of felt-tip pens, sponges and washing up liquids!). The creative solution, however, was to recognise the broader dimensions of the problem and provide the graffiti artists with somewhere else to exercise their skills and brighten up their local environment (a community whiteboard).

The 'think globally, act locally' approach is exemplified by the Sustrans (Sustainable Transport) *Safe Routes to Schools* project (Transport 2000 Trust 1999). This encourages schools to set up cycle routes in the locality and bike sheds in the playground to reduce the number of children travelling by car (and hence cut pollution, noise, accidents and congestion at the start and end of the school day). Children at three Leicester primary schools developed 'dinosaur footprint' signage for safe cycle trails, and another project involved children working with professional designers to develop 'gateway' signs warning drivers to slow down in local roads. York Steiner

School has involved primary-age children in designing bike sheds which were then built by adult volunteers. All of these initiatives have embodied the principles of active citizenship at a school level, while making connections to the wider issues of sustainable development.

The evidence from such projects, and the increasing availability of information from the Internet relating to eco-design, puts primary children in a strong position to make choices about materials, impact and appropriateness in their designs for local (e.g. the school playground), national (e.g. an exhibition centre) and international (e.g. emergency housing) needs. Participating in whole-class or whole-school initiatives to make changes can introduce children to notions such as democracy, representation and taking an active role in decision-making processes. But much of this work assumes that children are at an age when they are attaining some degree of autonomy and can begin to move outside the classroom environment, i.e. Key Stage 2 and beyond. What about younger children – how do we help them to get involved?

Active citizenship in the early years

Much of the literature on design and technology for young children (e.g. Siraj-Blatchford and MacLeod-Brudenell 1999) stresses the importance of *fantasy contexts* in helping them to identify needs and opportunities. Through the medium of stories, children in the early years can begin to empathise with characters and think about their needs within a broader context (Lewisham LEA 1999). The puppets project (Case Study 10, Chapter 3.2) enabled Year 1 children to appreciate the moral issues within traditional tales. The next step would be to think about how some of these issues could be addressed: what could Jack give the giant in return for the things he had taken? An alternative retelling of this tale – *Jim and the Beanstalk* by Raymond Briggs – introduces the idea that the giant has age-related needs: he's short-sighted, toothless and bald. Reception children at Holy Trinity Primary, Taunton made a giant papier mâché giant's head, then developed glasses, false teeth and a wig to fit it! Here is an example of a design brief for slightly older children, based on another character from a traditional tale:

The Troll's Bridge

This is the troll that gets those goats trampling all over his bridge. He is rather sick of this. He would really like you to make him a new bridge with somewhere to sleep peacefully *on the bridge*, but well away from goats and all other traffic. Troll's river is 60cm at its widest point. Troll himself is 8cm tall. Troll's job is to collect tolls (he is a toll troll). He would really like an automatic system to do the job for him.

Addressing this brief would involve the children in considering issues such as traffic congestion, noise and pollution. An example of young children getting involved in a real local environmental issue while designing homes for story characters is given below.

Case Study 13 – Homes for story characters (Year 1)

Introduction
This case study shows how the context of home can be used to address some wider issues about housing and shelter with young children. Changes to the local environment – in the form of a new housing estate – were used to think about different peoples' needs and wants in a home, and involved children in designing for imaginary characters. They also learned about the business and industry contexts of building and estate agency, engaging in buying and selling properties through role play.

Setting the scene
Bromley Heath Infants' School (South Gloucestershire) has recently adopted the QCA National Scheme of Work for Design and Technology (QCA/DfEE 1998), but design and technology subject leader Sarah Munday was keen to go beyond the basic requirements of Unit 1D 'Homes' in order to provide young children with a rich cross-curricular experience. For this reason she chose to take advantage of the new housing development being built locally to provide her Year 1 class with the opportunity of observing structures at various stages of completion, and consider ways in which the development would impact upon the local community. She was also anxious to provide children with a sense of the social setting within which homes are bought and sold, so an estate agency was set up in the classroom role-play area, complete with ICT-generated advertisements, index files, property descriptions and key tags. The project built on previous science work on materials – the Three Little Pigs – during which children had considered the most appropriate materials with which to construct homes. Sarah wanted children to make use of these skills and understandings in creating a new built environment. She planned to work on the project for an afternoon a week (using time designated for design and technology and art) and identified learning objectives from across the curriculum including PSHE and citizenship.

The teaching sequence

For the IEA Sarah took the class on a walk around the local area, identifying different types of houses and specific issues (for example, the children identified that the 'roads are too busy'). This raised their awareness of needs in the local area. During this first week the children made a visit to the local building site, where the site manager invited them into a show home. They all agreed that this was a 'good' thing for the local area, even though two older properties had been demolished to make room for the new development. The citizenship learning from this experience was that technology has winners (new home owners) and losers (people with homes demolished). When they got back to school they recorded features of buildings they had seen on their walk in observation drawings.

Over a period of several days children were sent home with a class camera to photograph their own home. Sarah attached the photos to a large map of the local area. This led to a discussion about their routes to school, and how these could be represented on maps. Children began writing descriptions of their own home for the class estate agency, which raised their awareness of the kinds of language used to persuade people to buy. Children produced advertisements for their homes using 'Tinydraw' software. Through acting as an estate agency, children developed an awareness of jobs done by people in the local area. Their economic understanding of buying and selling was also enhanced (see Chapter 3.2).

When children came to undertake the DMA, Sarah wanted them to be able to consider the particular needs of individuals, so set up a fantasy scenario in which children would design for story characters. They were to group the resulting models in a new housing development to be called 'Fairytale Land', while issues of access, space and traffic would be carefully considered. By asking children to work in mixed-ability pairs she hoped to develop the particular skills of cooperative working. Together, they developed prototypes using construction kits (LEGO etc.) to try out ideas, before producing annotated 'architects' drawings' of the home for their chosen character.

For a FPT, Sarah wanted to teach the class different ways of making a hinge for the opening door specified in the design brief. She made a concept board showing different methods of making a hinge which she demonstrated and discussed with the class. Next the children made choices of materials and shapes to form the basis for their homes. Two children discussed the best combination of tapering shapes to make the roof of Hansel and Gretel's house (Fig. 3.4.1). They had considered making see-through lollipop windows, but this was proving more difficult than expected. After an hour, Sarah gathered the children on the carpet for a joint problem-solving session. Each pair had to present their progress and discuss their problems with the wider group, who made suggestions about the way forward.

Having had experience of constructing their own homes, the children returned to the building site, this time with a set of questions to ask the site manager. They had been given architects' drawings of some of the new houses and wanted to know the reasons for some of the decisions. They then returned to school to place their completed models in the carefully planned Fairytale Land development. A plenary for shared evaluation was again an effective way of gathering everyone's thoughts about the outcome of the project.

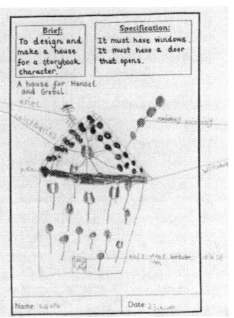

Figure 3.4.1 Design for a house for Hansel and Gretel

Discussion

Through the group evaluations children gained awareness that a group of people can take decisions together democratically and provide help and advice to individuals within it. Designing for story characters gave them a sense of the needs of different members of a community who are likely to live in a new housing development: access, safety, play, refuse collection etc. The deeper question underlying this project is why Britain – a country with a very low rate of population growth – needs new housing developments at all. With older children this question could have led to an analysis of social trends: more single people living alone, more families living in two locations. The topical debate between greenfield and brownfield sites for development would be a valuable one for children in upper Key Stage 2. This would need to consider and challenge the cultural preferences for our own front door and back garden, perhaps by looking at housing in Japan or other countries.

Summary and concluding thoughts

'Fairytale Land' is a phrase that fairly accurately describes many children's hopes for the future. The following is typical:

> I would like it if everybody would be happy and joyful, no violence and there would be no poverty ... it would be nice to have inventions which run by solar power. I would like to see the numbers of animals increase and see no more sea pollution.
>
> (Richard, aged 11, quoted in Hicks and Holden 1995: 74)

Such utopian visions stand in stark contrast to the cynicism and pessimistic fears about the future voiced by many adults. As primary educators we need to recapture some of this childlike vision and channel it into learning activities that question the status quo and create better futures. This might seem an impossible challenge in the current educational climate, but as we have shown throughout this book, creative teachers can work within curriculum constraints to address broader issues in their work with children. The case studies within this chapter – and in the book as a whole – represent in many ways standard good practice in primary design and technology, meeting the requirements of the National Curriculum and in many cases working within the QCA National Scheme of Work (QCA/DfEE 1998). They illustrate the effective teaching that we have taken as our baseline (Chapter 1.1). Yet in other respects they represent *creative* practice, in that the teachers have transcended curriculum limitations to release children to generate and explore future possibilities to improve their own lives and those of others within specific cultural contexts. This book has set out to move some of the visionary themes of the new curriculum – creativity, culture and citizenship – from the wings to centre stage. Here they can make their rightful contribution, through the powerful medium of design and technology, to primary education and all of our futures.

References

Appiah, L. (1999) 'Multicultural Citizenship', *Multicultural Teaching* 18(1), 20–23.

Arnot, M. and Dillabough, J. (eds) (2000) *Challenging Democracy – International Perspectives on Gender, Education and Citizenship*. London: Routledge/Falmer.

Ashcroft, K. and James, D. (eds) (1999) *The creative professional: Learning to teach 14–19 year olds*. London: Falmer Press.

Barlex, D. (2000) 'Preparing D&T for 2005 – Moving Beyond the Rhetoric', *Journal of Design and Technology Education* 5(1), 5–15.

Baxendall, M. (1985) *Patterns of Intention*. Yale: Yale University Press.

Benson, C. (1992) *Design and Technology at Key Stages 1 and 2*. York: Longman.

Benson, C. (2000) 'Ensuring Successful Curriculum Development in Primary Design and Technology', in Eggleston, J. (ed.) *Teaching and Learning Design and Technology: A Guide to Recent Research and its Applications*, 1–14. London: Continuum.

Benyon, J. and Mackay, H. (1992) *Technological Literacy and the Curriculum*. London: Falmer Press.

Bloomfield, P. (1998) 'The Challenge of Agenda 21 at Key Stages 1, 2 and 3', *Geography* 83(2), 97–104.

Broadbent, L. (1995) 'Making sense of the spiritual and moral', in Inman, S. and Buck, M. (eds) *Adding Value? Schools' responsibility for pupils' personal development*. Stoke-on-Trent: Trentham.

Browne, N. (ed.) (1991) *Science and Technology in the Early Years*. Buckingham: Open University Press.

Buck, M. and Inman, S. (1992) *Curriculum Guidance No 1 – Whole School Provision for Personal and Social Development: The Role of the Cross Curricular Elements*. London: Centre for Cross Curricular Initiatives, Goldsmiths' College.

Budgett-Meakin, C. (ed.) (1992) *Make the Future Work*. London: Longman.

Buzan, B. and Buzan, T. (1993) *The Mindmap Book*. London: BBC Books.

Claxton, G. (1998) *Hare Brain, Tortoise Mind: Why Intelligence Increases When You Think Less*. London: Fourth Estate.

Coates, D. and Rose, N. (1999) 'Design and Technology', in Bigger, S. and Brown, E. (eds) *Spiritual, Moral, Social and Cultural Education*. London: David Fulton Publishers.

Courtney-Clarke, M. (1990) *African Canvas*. New York: Rizzoli International Publications Incorporated.

Craft, A. (2000) *Creativity Across the Primary Curriculum: Framing and Developing Practice*. London: Routledge.

Crawford, K. (1999) 'New Labour, New Policies: Constructing a Discourse of Citizenship', *IACSEE Conference Proceedings*, Atlanta.

Crick, B. (1999) 'The Presuppositions of Citizenship Education', *Journal of Philosophy of Education* 33(3), 337–52.

Csikszentmihalyi, M. (1990) 'The Domains of Creativity', in Runco, M. A. and Albert, R. S. (eds) *Theories of Creativity*. London: Sage Publications.

Davies, D. (1991) 'Wild Designs', *The Big Paper* 11, 6.

Davies, D. (1992) 'Part of the Furniture', *The Big Paper* 16, 6.

Davies, D. (1996) 'Professional Design and Primary Children', *International Journal of Technology and Design Education* 6, 45–59.

Davies, D. (1997) 'The relationship between science and technology in the primary curriculum: alternative perspectives', *Journal of Design and Technology Education* 2(2), 101–11.

Davies, D. (2001) *Student Teachers' Beliefs about Science, Design & Technology: Influences on Planning for Activities in the Primary Classroom.* Unpublished Ph.D. thesis. Goldsmiths' College, University of London.

Davies, D., Rogers, M., Egan, B. and Martin, M. (2000) 'Carrying the Torch – Can Student Teachers Contribute to the Survival of Design and Technology in the Primary Curriculum?', in Kimbell, R. (ed.) *Design and Technology International Millennium Conference*, 47–52. Wellesbourne: Design and Technology Association (DATA).

Davies, L. (1999) 'Researching democratic understanding in primary school', *Research in Education* 61, 39–48.

Dearing, R. (1993) *The National Curriculum and its Assessment: Final Report.* London: School Curriculum and Assessment Authority (SCAA).

de Bono, E. (1970) *Lateral Thinking.* London: Ward Lock.

Dennick, R. (1992) 'Analysing multicultural and antiracist science', *School Science Review* 73(264), 79–88.

Department for Education and Employment (DfEE) (1995) *Looking at Values through Products and Applications.* London: DfEE.

Department for Education and Employment (DfEE)/Qualifications and Curriculum Authority (QCA) (1999a) *Design and Technology – The National Curriculum for England.* London: HMSO.

Department for Education and Employment (DfEE)/Qualifications and Curriculum Authority (QCA) (1999b) *Citizenship – The National Curriculum for England.* London: HMSO.

Department for Education and Employment (DfEE)/Qualifications and Curriculum Authority (QCA) (1999c) *The National Curriculum: Handbook for primary teachers in England.* London: HMSO.

Department for International Development (DfID) (2000) *Eliminating World Poverty: Making Globalisation Work for the Poor.* London: DfID.

Department of Education and Science (DES)/Welsh Office (WO) (1985) *Education for All: The Swann Report.* London: HMSO

Department of Education and Science (DES)/Welsh Office (WO) (1988) *The Education Reform Act.* London: HMSO.

Department of Education and Science (DES)/Welsh Office (WO) (1990) *Technology in the National Curriculum.* London: DES/WO.

Design and Technology Association (DATA) (n.d.) *Design & Technology* (pamphlet). Warwick: DATA.

Design and Technology Association (DATA) (1996) *The Design and Technology Primary Co-ordinator's File.* Wellesbourne: DATA.

Design and Technology Association (DATA) (1997) *Planning into Practice.* Wellesbourne: DATA.

Design Council (2001) *The Big Zipper: How to Unzip Your Creativity.* London: Design Council.

Dixon, A. (1999) 'Preconceptions and Practice in Primary Citizenship Education', *Forum* 41(1), 2–10.

Durbin G., Morris S. and Wilkinson, S. (1990) *A Teacher's Guide to Learning from Objects.* London: English Heritage.

Dust, K. (1999) *Motive, Means and Opportunity: Creativity Research Review.* London: National Endowment for Science, Technology and the Arts (NESTA).

Eisner, E. (1989) 'Structure and Magic in Discipline-Based Art Education', in Thistlewood, D. (ed.) *Critical Studies in Art and Design Education.* London: Longman.

Fisher, R. (1998) *Teaching Thinking: Philosophical Enquiry in the Classroom.* London: Cassell.

Franklin, R. (1986) *The Rights of Children.* Oxford: Basil Blackwell.

Frost, J. (1997) *Creativity in Primary Science.* Milton Keynes: Open University Press.

Fryer, L. (1996) *Creative Teaching and Learning.* London: Chapman.

Gardner, H. (1983) *Frames of Mind: The Theory of Multiple Intelligences.* London: Heinemann.

Gardner, H. (1990) *Art Education and Human Development.* Los Angeles: Getty Centre for Education in the Arts.

Gardner, P. (1994) 'Representations of the Relationship between Science and Technology in the Curriculum', *Studies in Science Education* 24(1), 1–13.

Garvey, G. and Quinlan, A. (2000) 'Evaluating Design and Technology', in Sefton-Green, J. and Sinker, R. (eds) *Evaluating Creativity: Making and Learning by Young People*, 43–69. London: Routledge.

Gibson, H. and Backus, J. (2001) 'Presuppositions of moral and political action: Does the citizenship curriculum 'contain' the expression of end games that may follow from debate?' Unpublished conference paper presented at *Diverse Citizenship,* University of North London, 30 March 2001.

Gill, D. and Levidov, L. (1987) *Anti-racist Science Teaching.* London: Free Association Books.

Gilroy, B. (1986) *There Ain't No Black in the Union Jack.* London: Hutchinson.

Goggin, P. and Lawler, T. (1998) 'Sustainability and design and technology in schools', *Journal of Design and Technology Education* 3(2), 106–12.

Goleman, D. (1994) *Emotional Intelligence – Why it can matter more than IQ.* London: Bloomsbury.

Green, A. (1997) 'Core Skills, General Education and Unification in Post-16 Education', in Hodgson, A. and Spours, K. (eds) *Dearing and Beyond.* London: Kogan Page.

Halliwell, G. (1993) 'Teacher creativity and teacher education', in Bridges, D. and Kerry, T. (eds) *Developing Teachers Professionally: Reflections for Initial and In-service Trainers.* London: Routledge.

Hammond, S. (1997) 'From source to sale: developing an education pack', *Journal of Design and Technology Education* 2(1), 53–60.

Hansard Society (1978) *Political Education and Political Literacy.* London: Hansard Society.

Harland, J., Kinder, K. and Hartley, K. (1995) *Executive Summary – Arts in their View.* Reading: National Foundation for Educational Research (NFER).

Harrington, D. M. (1990) 'The Ecology of Human Creativity: A psychological perspective', in Runco, M. A. and Albert, R. S. (eds) *Theories of Creativity.* London: Sage Publications.

Hicks, D. (1995) 'Citizenship for Today and Tomorrow', in Inman, S. and Buck, M. (eds) *Adding Value? Schools' responsibility for pupils' personal development.* Stoke-on-Trent: Trentham.

Hicks, D. (1999) 'Praxis of the Heart: Reflections on Education for the New Century', *Fifth UNESCO-ASCEID International Conference,* Bangkok, 13–16 December.

Hicks, D. and Holden, C. (1995) *Visions of the Future: Why We Need to Teach for Tomorrow.* Stoke-on-Trent: Trentham.

Howe, A. (1999) 'A Visual Literacy Strategy – Why not?', *Journal of Design and Technology Education* 4(3), 215–22.

Hyland, T. and Johnson, S. (1998) 'Of Cabbages and Key Skills: exploding the mythology of core transferable skills in post-school education', *Journal of Further and Higher Education* 22(2), 163–72.

Jarvis, T. and Rennie, L. (2000) *Helping Children Understand Science and Technology.* Leicester: SCI Centre.

Johnston, J. (1996) *Early Explorations in Science.* Buckingham: Open University Press.

Kane, T. (1990) 'Making Musical Instruments at Key Stage 1', *Design and Technology Teaching* 22(2), 68–73.

Kelly, A. (ed.) (1987) *Science for Girls.* Milton Keynes: Open University Press.

Kimbell, R. (2000) 'Creativity in Crisis', *Journal of Design and Technology Education* 5(3), 206–11.

Kimbell, R., Stables, K., Wheeler, T., Wozniak, A. and Kelly, A. V. (1991) *The Assessment of Performance in Design and Technology.* London: Evaluation and Monitoring Unit (EMU), School Examinations and Assessment Council (SEAC).

Kirkup, G. and Smith Keller, L. (eds) (1992) *Inventing Women: Science, Technology and Gender.* Cambridge: Polity Press with the Open University.

Layton, D. (1992) 'Values in Design and Technology', in Budgett-Meakin, C. (ed.) *Make the Future Work.* London: Longman.

Layton, D. (1993) *Technology's Challenge to Science Education.* Milton Keynes: Open University Press.

Layton, D. (1995) 'Constructing and Reconstructing School Technology in England and Wales', *International Journal of Technology and Design Education* 5, 89–118.

Lewisham LEA (1999) *Find that Book: Making links between literacy and the broader curriculum.* London: Lewisham LEA.

Linton, T. (1990) 'A Child's-Eye View of Economics', in Ross, A. (ed.) *Economic and Industrial Awareness in the Primary School.* London: PNL Press.

Loeb, H., Slight, P. and Stanley, N. (1993) *Designs We Live By.* Corsham: National Society for Education in Art and Design.

Lowenfeld, V. T. and Britten, W. (1975) *Creative and Mental Growth.* New York: Collier MacMillan.

Maiteney, P. and Wade, R. (1999) 'Citizenship Education', in Bigger, S. and Brown, E. (eds) (1999) *Spiritual, Moral, Social and Cultural Education.* London: David Fulton Publishers.

Matthews, B. and Davies, D. (1999) 'Changing children's images of scientists: can teachers make a difference?', *School Science Review* 80(293), 79–85.

McCormick, R. (1999) 'Capability Lost and Found? The Maurice Brown Memorial Lecture', *Journal of Design and Technology Education* 4(1), 5–13.

McCormick, R., Davidson, M., and Levinson, R. (1995) 'Making Connections: students' scientific understanding of electric currents in design and technology', in Smith, J. S. (ed.) *IDATER 95*. Loughborough: Loughborough University of Technology.

McGarry, A. (1992) 'Appropriate Technology', in Budgett-Meakin, C. (ed.) *Make the Future Work*. London: Longman.

McGuinness, C. (1999) *From Thinking Skills to Thinking Classrooms* – Research report **1**, 15 (April). Sudbury: Department for Education and Employment (DfEE).

McMahon, K. (1999) 'Perceptions of Science and Gender in a Key Stage 2 Class', *The Redland Papers* 7(Spring), 53–68.

Mulberg, C. (1992) 'Technological Myths in Education', in Budgett-Meakin, C. (ed.) *Make the Future Work*. London: Longman.

National Advisory Committee on Creative and Cultural Education (NACCCE) (1999) *All Our Futures: Creativity, Culture and Education*. Sudbury: Department for Education and Employment (DfEE).

National Curriculum Council (NCC) (1990a) *Curriculum Guidance 3: The Whole Curriculum*. York: NCC.

National Curriculum Council (NCC) (1990b) *Curriculum Guidance 8: Education for Citizenship*. York: NCC.

National Curriculum Council (NCC) (1990c) *Curriculum Guidance 4 : Education for Economic and Industrial Understanding*. York: NCC.

National Curriculum Council (NCC) (1991) *Planning Design and Technology at Key Stages 1 and 2*. York: NCC.

National Curriculum Design and Technology Working Group (1988) *Interim Report*. London: Department of Education (DES)/Welsh Office (WO).

Office for Standards in Education and Training (OFSTED) (1993) *Framework for the Inspection of Schools*. London: HMSO.

Office for Standards in Education and Training (OFSTED) (1998) *Standards in Design and Technology 1996 –1997*. London: OFSTED.

Office for Standards in Education and Training (OFSTED) (1999a) *Standards in Design and Technology 1997–1998*. London: OFSTED.

Office for Standards in Education and Training (OFSTED) (1999b) *A Review of Primary Schools in England, 1994–1998*. London: The Stationery Office.

Office for Standards in Education and Training (OFSTED) (2001A) *Standards in Subjects 1999–2000*. London: OFSTED.

Ollerenshaw, C. and Ritchie, R. (1997) *Primary Science: Making it Work*, 2nd edn. London: David Fulton Publishers.

Orr, D. (1993) 'Schools for the 21st Century', *Resurgence* **160**, 16–19.

Osler, A. (1999) 'Citizenship, democracy and political literacy', *Multicultural Teaching* **18**(1), 12–15, 29.

Oxfam (1997) *A Curriculum for Global Citizenship*. Oxford: Oxfam.

Panel for Education for Sustainable Development (1998) *Education for Sustainable Development in the Schools Sector*. London: Council for Environmental Education, Development Education Association, RSPB and WWF-UK.

Pascall, D. (1992) *Notes of a speech at the Royal Society of Arts* (20 November 1992). London: Royal Society of Arts (RSA).

Paxman, J. (1998) *The English: a Portrait of a People*. London: Penguin.

Piaget, J. (1932) *The Moral Judgement of the Child*. London: Routledge and Kegan Paul.

Qualifications and Curriculum Authority (QCA) (1997) *Food in Schools: Ideas*. London: QCA.

Qualifications and Curriculum Authority (QCA) (1998) *Education for Citizenship and the Teaching of Democracy in Schools* (The Crick Report). London: QCA.

Qualifications and Curriculum Authority (QCA) Working Party on Sustainable Development (1999) *Sustainable Development in the National Curriculum*. London: QCA.

Qualifications and Curriculum Authority (QCA)/Department for Education and Employment (DfEE) (1998) *Design and Technology : A scheme of work for Key Stages 1 and 2*. London: QCA.

Qualifications and Curriculum Authority (QCA)/Department for Education and Employment (DfEE) (2000a) *Curriculum Guidance for the Foundation Stage*. London: QCA.

Qualifications and Curriculum Authority (QCA)/Department for Education and Employment (DfEE) (2000b) *Art and Design: A scheme of work for Key Stages 1 and 2*. London: QCA.

Qualifications and Curriculum Authority (QCA)/Department for Education and Employment (DfEE) (2001) *Citizenship: A scheme of work for Key Stages 1 and 2*. London: QCA.

Raney, K. (1999) 'Visual Literacy and the Art Curriculum', *Journal of Art and Desig*
41–7.

Rennie, L. and Jarvis, T. (1994) *Helping Children Understand Technology*. Perth: Curt

Review Group for Design and Technology (1992) *Technology for Ages 5–16: Proposals*
of State for Education and the Secretary of State for Wales. London: HMSO.

Ritchie, R. (2001) *Design and Technology: a Process for Learning*, 2nd edn. London:
Publishers.

Rogers, M. (1997) 'Development education through design and technology'. in Inman, S.
W. (eds) *Development Education within Initial Teacher Education: shaping a better futu*
OXFAM.

Rogers, M. and Davies, D. (1999) 'What has happened to primary design and technology? ᴟ ᴟᴄᴎ
teachers in search of a foundation subject'. Unpublished paper given at *BERA 99*, University of
Sussex, 2–5 September 1999.

Ross, A. (1992) 'Promoting the Enterprise Culture or developing a critique of the political economy?
Directions for economic and industrial understanding', in Hutchings, M. and Wade, W. (eds)
Developing Economic and Industrial Understanding in the Primary School. London: PNL Press.

Rousseau, J. (1911) *Emile*. London: Dent.

Schumacher, E. F. (1973) *Small is Beautiful*. London: Abacus/Sphere Books.

Schweinhart, L. J. and Weikart, D. P. (1997) *A Summary of Significant Benefits: the High/Scope Perry*
Pre-school Study through age 2–7. Ypsilanti: High/Scope Press.

Seberry, B. (1996) 'Technology in the primary school: the contribution of a cultural framework',
Journal of Design and Technology Education 1(3), 249–55.

Sefton-Green, J. and Sinker, R. (eds) (2000) *Evaluating Creativity: Making and Learning by Young*
People. London: Routledge.

Selwood, S., Clive, S. and Irving, D. (1995) *An Enquiry into Young People and Art Galleries*. London:
Art & Society.

Sharp, K. and Dust, K. (1997) *Artists in Schools. A Handbook for teachers and artists*. Reading:
National Foundation for Educational Research (NFER).

Siraj-Blatchford, J. (1994): 'Values in design and technology: an anti-racist dimension', *Design and*
Technology Teaching 27, 57–60.

Siraj-Blatchford, J. (1996) *Learning Technology, Science and Social Justice*. Nottingham: Education
Now Publishing.

Siraj-Blatchford, J. and MacLeod-Brudenell, I. (1999) *Supporting Science, Design and Technology in*
the Early Years. Buckingham: Open University Press.

Snow, C. P. (1959) *The Two Cultures: A Second Look*. Cambridge: Cambridge University Press.

Solomon, J. (1995) *Using Stories for Science and Technology*. Hatfield: ASE Publications.

Starkey, H. (ed.) (1991) *The Challenge of Human Rights Education*. London: Cassell.

Supple, C. (1999) 'Ideals for Citizenship Education', *Multicultural Teaching* 18(1), 16–19.

Taylor, R. (1986) *Educating for Art. Critical response and development*. Harlow: Longman.

Teacher Training Agency (TTA) (1998a) *National Standards for Headteachers*. London: TTA.

Teacher Training Agency (TTA) (1998b) *National Standards for Subject Leaders*. London: TTA.

Thomas, J. C. and Carroll, J. M. (1979) 'The Psychological Study of Design', *Design Studies* 1(1),
45–54.

Transport 2000 Trust (1999) *A Safer Journey to School*. London: Department for Education and
Employment (DfEE).

Tribe, J. (1996) 'Core Skills: a critical examination', *Educational Review* 48(1), 13–27.

United Nations Educational, Scientific and Cultural Organisation (UNESCO) (1978) *Declaration on*
Race and Prejudice. Geneva: UNESCO.

Watts, M. (1991) *Problem Solving in School Science*. Milton Keynes: Open University Press.

White, P. (1999) 'Political Education in the Early Years: the place of civic virtues', *Oxford Review of*
Education 25(1–2), 59–70.

Williams, P. and Jinks, D. (1985) *Design and Technology 5–12*. Lewes: Falmer Press.

Wilson, J. (1990) *A New Introduction to Moral Education*. London: Cassell.

Winston, J. (1998) *Drama, Narrative and Moral Education*. London: Falmer Press.

Woods, P. (1996) 'The Good Times, Creative Teaching in Primary School', *Education* 24(2), 3–12.

World Commission on Environment and Development (1987) *Our Common Future* (The
Brundtland Report). Oxford: Oxford University Press.

Yeomans, M. (1996) 'Creativity in Art and Science: A Personal View', *Journal of Art and Design*
Education 15(3), 241–50.

Index

active citizenship 7, 132,
  163–4, 169, 174
active participation, 125, 129, 165
aesthetics
  and beauty 144
  and spirituality 143
  awareness 40
  children's 51
  evaluating 42
  knowledge of 25
  prevalent aesthetics 93,
  understanding of 42
  value judgements about 70
Agenda 21, 130, 132, 170
air-raid shelters 81, 120
antiracist approaches to design
  and technology 7, 72, 104
  117–8, 122, 128–9
apprenticeship 7, 52, 122
appropriate technologies 3
art
  art critics 14
  art curriculum 40, 71
  art education 38, 41
  knowledge from 25
  relationship with design and
  technology 79, 87–103
art students 56
artefacts (*see* evaluating artefacts)
  collections of 113
  handling 40
  historical 120,
  making 58, 101, 121
  modelled 96
  presenting 107
  religious 116
artist in residence 50
artistic skills 155
artists 40, 50, 52, 88, 92, 93
arts
  and creativity 20, 50
  relationship with design and
  technology 7, 64, 71,
  87–103, 108, 122
assessment 4, 22, 37, 139, 158,
  162

behaviour management 27
beliefs 14, 64, 67-8, 128
bread making 28, 49, 114–5
buildings 32, 50, 106, 176
built environment 175

CD ROMs 108, 110–11,
  155–6, 158-9
Cezanne 93
children's fiction 101–2
children's interests 24, 49
Christmas 26, 90, 93, 102,
  113, 116, 144

citizenship (*see also* global
  citizenship) 3, 5–7, 125–178
  and culture 67, 84, 108,
  112, 125
  and democracy 149–50
  and key skills 156–3
  and PSHE 126
  and social awareness 151
  and sustainable futures 164
  79
  and thinking skills 155–6
  classic tradition of 127
  liberal democratic tradition of
  128–9
  liberal republican model of
  130
  National Scheme of Work,
  148, 170
  progression in 134–5
citizens
  of the school 131
  of the world 133
civics 127
computers, 3, 103 (*see also* ICT)
concept board 176
construction kit 23
costumes 89–91, 98–9, 102,
  116
craftworkers 93
creative arts 87
creative development 18, 20, 22
  3, 35–6, 59, 107
creative ecosystem 16
creative growth 6, 11, 15–17
creative partnerships 52
creative process 6, 14, 40, 45,
  50
creative school 31
creative teachers 178
creative teaching 6, 17, 30,
  31–3, 35, 78
creative thinking 6, 47, 53–6
creative thought 17, 18, 20,
  36
creativity 11–59
  and culture 63, 91–3,
  100–101
  and science and technology
  74
  and social awareness 151
  and spirituality 143–4
  and supportive classroom
  ethos 28, 30, 32, 54
  right environment for
  15–16, 27
Crick report 127–8, 137, 170
criteria,
  for designing and making
  29, 39–40, 42, 80
  for evaluaing making 44

for evaluating teaching 45–6
for testing 78
for sorting 161
critical studies 40–1
critical thinking 37, 93, 133
cross-curricular approaches 5,
  41, 76, 127, 134, 142,
  154, 156, 175
cultural contexts 7, 60, 63, 84,
  104, 178
cultural diversity 5, 69, 105,
  122, 128
cultural education 7, 63, 66,
  67, 74, 86, 104, 105, 120,
  122
cultural perspectives 5
culture 60–122
  and creativity 12, 2
  of collaboration 31
  supportive 27
  and citizenship 125, 128,
  130, 137, 140, 142, 157,
  168, 179
Curriculum 2000 (*see also*
  National Curriculum) 5, 7,
  67–8, 133–8, 147, 151,
  154–6, 163, 165–6
Curriculum Guidance 23
cutting skills, 22–3, 57–8, 90,
  160, 165

dance 20, 52
DATA 20, 42
dawning realism 38
Dearing review 19
democratic participation 127
democratic structures 135
design and make assignments
  (DMAs) 4, 39, 57, 80–81,
  83, 131–2, 142, 144, 146,
  162, 156, 157, 160, 176
Design and Technology
  Association 20
design brief 15, 39, 43–4,
  92–3, 98, 131, 133, 146,
  152, 156, 174–6
Design Museum 140
design process 50, 138, 170
designers (*see also* design related
  professionals) 55, 56, 70,
  76, 139, 147
  and sustainability 167
  children as designers 81,
  92–3
  children's encounters with
  50–2, 90, 98, 100, 173
  processes used by 152
designer's education 21
designer's intentions 41, 141–4
design-related professionals 50, 52

device knowledge   155
differentiation   27, 58, 111, 146
digital camera   44, 96, 101, 156
digital photograph   121
Diwali   65, 116
drama   70, 87–8, 91, 99, 103,
    147
drawing (see sketching)   4, 24,
    25, 58, 80, 162

Early Learning Goals   22–3, 37,
    77
early years (see also reception) 5,
    38, 57–8, 174
Easter   96, 116
eco-design   167-8, 174
eco-logging   167
Edison   11, 119
effective teaching   30, 33, 35,
    136
egocentrism   145
Eid   116
electrical components/circuits
    59, 100, 155, 158
electrical control   158
email   121
emotional development   145
emotional intelligence   151
enquiry skills   155
environment   164
    and sustainability   135, 168
    and values   43, 69–70
    impact on   82-3, 167
    local   107
    school   131
environmental issues   70
environmental awareness   84,
    165, 172–4
environmental catastrophe   2
environmental education   166
environments   50, 143
ethnic minority   106
ethnicity   65, 68
ethnocentric   119
ethnocentricity   84
ethos (see creativity and e.)   69,
    131
Eurocentric   106
European   66
European Convention on Human
    Rights   147
European   65
evaluation   92, 132
    and digital camera   44
    criteria for   40, 43
    of children's outcomes   79,
        177
    of existing artefacts, designs
        and products   33, 41–3, 48,
        50, 57, 72, 79, 90, 107,
        114, 120, 141, 159, 177
    of teaching   45–6
    of progress   24
    progression in   38–9
    self-evaluation   36
    skills of   37, 154, 156

exhibitions   50
extrinsic motivation   21

fabrics (see textiles)   77, 89, 99
family   65, 69
feminist   128
festival   114, 116, 144, 160,
    161
festivals   65, 103, 116
finishing   25
focused practical tasks (FPTs)   4,
    25, 57, 59, 80–81, 111,
    144, 160, 162–3, 176
food   4, 16, 28–9, 59, 76, 84,
    91, 102, 106–7, 114–16,
    119–20, 153, 160–3
formative assessments   22
foundation stage   25, 49
Foundation Stage   20, 23, 37,
    77
foundation subjects   40
future (see also sustainable
    futures)
    preferred future   171
    visions of   1–3, 6, 59, 71,
        83, 85, 121, 147, 152,
        154, 156, 160, 164, 166
future (children's hopes)   178
future (children's views)   165

gallery   52
Gallileo   75
gatekeeper   14
gatekeepers   14, 15, 37
gender   65, 84, 86, 152
generative thinking   45, 49, 53,
    56, 58-9
generative thought
    genius   11, 12, 16
geography   5, 53, 136, 172,
    173
'girl-friendly' technology   84
global citizenship   132, 141
global economy   2
globalisation   2, 133
governing body   131
government   2, 31, 34, 35,
    125–6, 128, 129, 132,
    135, 149, 155, 157
governors   1, 32, 172
group work   39, 111

Hanukkah   116
head teachers   31
health and safety (see also hygiene
    and safety)   29, 44, 158
hidden' curriculum   131
high-attaining children   112
history   40–1, 51, 53, 76, 84,
    105–6, 113, 119–20, 168,
    171
Hogarth   95
holistic   22, 26, 139
human rights   69, 147-8, 153,
    170
hygiene   26, 31, 160-1

ICT   58, 98, 101, 121, 142,
    157, 158, 175
identify needs   48, 174
identities (cultural)   64–6
illumination   14–15
imagination   3, 6, 12, 14, 59
imaginative   12, 20, 21, 49
incubation   14
inequality   2, 114, 117, 166
information technology   2, 4,
    102
Information-processing skills
    155
interactionist (model of science
    and technology)   75–9, 81,
    86–7
Intermediate Technology Group
    133
internet   66, 109, 110, 155,
    156, 158, 171, 174
intrinsic motivation   22
investigative and evaluative
    activities (IEAs)   4, 25, 41,
    43, 50, 80, 81, 120,
    140–1, 150, 153, 176

Joseph's Coat   39, 41, 92

Key Skills   156
Knowledge and Understanding of
    the World   23
knowledge economy   2

language   22–3, 38, 40, 43, 51,
    65, 68, 84, 110, 140, 176
lateral thinking   53
Learning Across the Curriculum 6
Learning Through Landscapes
    Trust   171
Lifelong Learning Project   158
Literacy   23, 41, 75, 145–6, 171
local environment   49, 175
local issues   83

mathematics (see also numeracy)
    40, 85
mechanical   4, 59, 155
mechanisms   24–5, 57, 106, 159
mentor   15–16
mini-enterprise   4, 152
modelling   50, 83, 90, 92, 93
monitoring   45-6
moral awareness   144
moral development   147
moral education   144
motivation   21, 23-4, 32, 39
multicultural education   2, 7,
    65, 71–2, 84, 102, 104-7,
    114–22, 129, 161, 163
multiculturalism   64, 117
multiethnic   2
museum   52
Museum of London   120
music   20, 55, 71, 87–8, 96–7,
    101-3, 108–9, 113, 116,
    170

musical instruments   49, 72, 77,
      97, 109-13, 118, 121,
      144, 155

National Advisory Committee for
      Creative and Cultural
      Education (NACCCE)   7,
      12-15, 30, 33–4, 52, 64,
      73–4, 88, 104, 106, 122
National Curriculum   4, 19, 37,
      40, 53, 67, 69, 75–6, 82,
      85, 93, 105, 117, 126–27,
      134, 142-3, 150, 164–5,
      178
National Endowment for Science,
      Technology and the Arts   52
National Forum for Values in
      Education   127
National Gallery   96
National Primary Trust   31
National Scheme of Work for
      design and technology (see
      also units of work)   4, 28,
      34, 79, 91, 131, 141, 147,
      152, 175, 178,
      and art 93
National Scheme of Work for
      citizenship   132, 170
National Standards for
      Headteachers   32
new technologies   71, 88, 102,
      103
non-threatening atmosphere   45
Numeracy (see also mathematics)
      75
nursery   25–6

OFSTED   4, 5, 32, 34, 45, 142
open ended questioning   41
open-mindedness   21, 105
opera   51, 52, 88, 97-100, 102,
      103, 152
originality   6, 13, 19, 27, 29
Oxfam   114, 133, 141

parents   21, 24, 26, 28, 31–3,
      44, 52, 54, 83, 91, 96–7
      116, 129, 131, 150, 155,
      162, 171
peer pressure   54, 150
Personal, Social and Health
      Education (PSHE)   109,
      114, 126, 134, 138, 149,
      158, 175
photo frame   57
photographs   55, 96, 98, 102,
      121, 161, 176
Picasso   92, 93
planning   6, 25–6, 30, 76, 79,
      85, 106, 115, 119, 131,
      138, 146, 162, 164, 167,
      172–3
play (see also, role-play)   20,
      22–4, 45, 134, 148,
      and creativity   12

and ideas   51, 53, 56
      producing a p.   90–91
playfulness   21, 24
playground   24, 33, 57, 65, 68,
      70, 102, 131-2, 161,
      171–74
pollution   71
popular culture   71, 88, 102,
      108
pottery   107
poverty   2, 101, 112–13, 118,
      165, 178
professional development   34,
      45
progression   37, 57, 134, 145,
      167
      in active participation   169
prototype   4, 159, 170
puppets   91–2, 113, 145–6,
      153, 174

Qualifications and Curriculum
      Authority Scheme of Work
      for Design and Technology,
      (see National Scheme of
      Work, see also units of work)
      questioning   7, 42, 108,
      133, 153

racist   72, 104, 117–19, 128
reasoning skills   155
reception   22, 174
relationships   43, 50, 52, 65,
      68–9, 128, 150–1
religion   68, 148
religious education   40, 136,
      142
risk taking   27, 30, 34, 147
role model   16, 50
role-play   55, 153, 175
role-play area   176
Royal Opera House   96

safety   99
sandwich   26, 28–9, 44
school community   32
science   7, 25, 40, 53, 70, 97
      and technology education
      117
      women in   119
      and technology   73–86, 156,
      158–9
      cultural impact of   70,
self-esteem   38, 105
self-image   5, 16, 134
set design   98
sketches   98–9, 171
sketching   50, 92
social awareness   150
social class   65
social constructivist   4
social justice   128, 135
society   1
special educational needs   31
spiritual development   143

spiritual dimension   67, 69,
      116, 142–44, 153
spiritual education   143
stereotypes   66
stories (as a starting point)   174
subject leaders   1, 32, 45
supportive environment   45
sustainability   117, 130, 132,
sustainable development   3,
      164–7, 174
sustainable development
      education   169
sustainable futures   2, 7, 126,
      136, 171
sustainable growth   166
Sustrans (Sustainable Transport)
      Safe Routes to Schools
      project   173
Swann Report   105

tape recorder   102
Tate Modern   93
Teachers in Development
      Education   133
technological awareness   138
technological development   2, 3,
      7, 88, 107, 136, 139
technological futures   164
technological literacy   5, 139
technological society   3, 105,
      139
technologists   12, 50, 75–6,
      83–5, 88, 119, 139, 147
textiles, (see fabrics)   4, 59, 90,
      95, 108, 145
The Citizenship Foundation
      128
thinking skills   47, 48, 53,
      154–5, 163
torches   79–82, 120, 155
transferable skills   154
Travel buddies'   121

units of work   28, 34, 79, 92,
      13, 131, 144, 160, 165,
      168
USA   2
values   2, 68–9
      shared values   14, 31, 64,
      88, 129

verification   14–15
video camera   97, 102
visual literacy   5, 40–1, 88, 96,
      126
visual world   41

web pages   103
web sites   84, 103, 111
women   12
      achievements of   84–5,
      118,
      and citizenship   127, 128
wood   22, 23, 111

Printed in the United Kingdom
by Lightning Source UK Ltd.
109919UKS00002B/277-280